Find 'em & Keep 'em

How to Use Traditional and Online Media to Acquire and Retain Your Most Valuable Business Asset

by

Russ Holder

www.RussHolder.com

BEP Business Excellence Press

Find 'em & Keep 'em: How to Use Traditional and Online Media to Acquire and Retain Your Most Valuable Business Asset

Disclaimer and Terms of Use: This publication is designed to provide accurate and authoritative information with regard to the subject matter covered. It is sold with the understanding that the publisher is not engaged in rendering legal, accounting, or other professional advice. If legal advice or other expert assistance is required, the services of a competent professional should be sought.

> —From a *Declaration of Principles* jointly adopted by a Committee of the American Bar Association and a Committee of Publishers and Associations.

ISBN: 978-1-939315-15-1

Table of Contents

Chapter 1: Creating Your Own Effective Advertisements

"If you think advertising doesn't pay – there are 30 mountains in Colorado higher than Pikes Peak. Can you name one?

- Anonymous

Advertising is a topic that many business owners find confusing and frustrating. When used correctly, advertising can be the most profitable marketing tool a small business has. Most often, though, advertising is used incorrectly, taking huge chunks out of a small business's budget, scaring many business owners from ever trying again. Some business owners may start thinking that advertising doesn't even pay.

The goal of this chapter is to take the mystery out of advertising. I want to help you understand how you can make it work for your business or professional practice. By the time you finish this chapter you will be able to put together a great ad that produces an immediate, measureable response from your target audience.

Ad'-ver-tiz'-ing: *Advertising is nothing more than presenting a self-serving benefit to your target audience. Advertising is making a successful sales presentation to the right people and convincing them to purchase or to ask for more information.*

RULE #1: Always Use Direct Response Advertising

If your goal is to increase sales, remember the first rule of effective advertising: **Always use direct response advertising.** As the name indicates, direct response ads are designed to produce an immediate response or action. It asks the audience to call, visit, or purchase.

Direct response advertising is salesmanship in print or on the air. It gives the targeted prospect specific reasons why your company, product, or service is better than our competitions. Direct response advertising overcomes objections, answers, questions, and promises benefits. Because direct response advertising compels the audience to take action, you can easily measure the effectiveness of the ad.

You must assume that the prospect doesn't care at all about your business or motives. You must assume the prospect only cares about the benefits your product or service will give them. How will your product or service save them time, money or effort?

The opposite of direct response is institutional or image advertising. The goal of institutional advertising is simply to keep your name in front of the public. It tells the public how wonderful you are. Institutional advertising does not produce measurable results.

A common misconception about institutional advertising is that it's good when people remember your name, like your ads, or even find them entertaining. Wrong! Well, maybe it's not bad, but it doesn't make you money. Let me give you a couple of examples:

The first is from the Chevrolet division of General Motors Corporation, which invested $100 million into their "Heartbeat of America" campaign back in the mid 1980's. Everyone in the country could sing the jingle. In fact, the campaign was so successful that the President of the ad agency and the Vice President of Marketing for GM were featured on the cover of Advertising Age, the industry bible, for winning the Cleo Award. The Cleo Award is the equivalent of the Academy Award in the advertising industry. Guess what? Sales for GM went down 20%.

The second is the most popular advertising campaign in the history of the Wendy's fast food restaurant chain was the famous "Where's The Beef" campaign. People still remember it almost 30 years later. Testing proved it to have a very high recall among consumers. But it didn't sell any hamburgers. It proved to be one of the most unsuccessful campaigns Wendy's has ever run.

Stay away from institutional advertising!

RULE #2: Only advertise when your message will be heard by a high concentration of the people you want to reach.

To identify where you should advertise and what media you should use, come up with a profile of your ideal customer. Research demographics and psychographics to determine where they live, what other products and services they buy, their level of affluence, etc. Do they commute to work? If so, drive time radio may be good. Do they read the newspaper or magazines? What medium does your target market use the most? It is very important to separate the masses from your target market.

Analyzing your existing customer base is the easiest way to identify the specifics of your target market.

RULE #3: Use the AIDA formula.

What you say and how you say it is just as important as where you say it. The AIDA principle that we've all heard about proves true in successful advertising.

To be effective, your ads need to have these four elements:

A – Grab the audience's *attention*. A compelling headline catches the attention of your target audience and motivates them to continue to read, listen, or watch the rest of your message.

I – Deepen the audience's *interest*. Tell the audience about the wonderful benefits they will receive from your product or service.

D – Increase the *desire* of your prospect. Explain the needs your target market would like to have filled. Then explain how your product or service fills those needs.

A – Motivate the prospect to take some specific *action*. Tell your prospect exactly what steps to take.

RULE #4: Always use headlines.

The headline is the most important element in your advertisement. It is essentially the advertisement for your advertisement. Why is this? People scan headlines as they look for something that interests them. On average, five times as many people read the headlines as do the rest of the ad.

The purpose of a headline is to grab your prospect's attention. It should target exactly whom you want to reach - your target market. It should tell the prospect the essence of what you're trying to say in the rest of the ad.

You should also incorporate your selling promise into your headline. Make the promise as specific and desirable to the prospect as possible. A good headline explains how the prospect can save, gain, or accomplish something beneficial through the use of your product or service. I once read about a simple change in a headline that made a 5,000% difference in the pulling results of an ad.

Here are some guidelines for writing powerful headlines:

- Appeal to the reader's self-interest.

- Try to inject news into the headline. The most powerful words you can use in headlines are free, new, you, how to, introducing, now, and announcing.

- Stay away from tricky, or cute, headlines. No puns, literary illusions, or other obscurities. Cute does not sell!

- Do not use negatives in headlines. For example, if you write that your pizza contains no preservatives, many readers will miss the negative and go away thinking that your pizza does contain preservatives.

- Avoid blind headlines – the kind which mean nothing unless you read the body copy underneath them. Remember, people scan headlines so they can decide which body text will interest them.

You must use headlines not only in print ads, but in all promotional communications with customers. It can be the opening sentence or paragraph you use in a radio or TV commercial, or a sales letter. It can be the first words you or your sales staff uses in a sales presentation.

RULE #5: Focus on the benefits to your customer.

Answer this question from your customer's perspective: "What's in it for me?"

It is important that you understand your prospects don't care about all of the wonderful features or your product or service. Many don't even care if you can save them money. And, no, they probably don't care if they are helping you grow your business. They only care about one thing: What's in it for me? What unique benefit, advantage, or enhancement you offer that someone else doesn't offer.

Customers want the benefits of your product or service and how it can help them improve their lives. Make a list of all the benefits your product or service provides. What about your product or service is most likely to get the attention of the audience you are trying to reach? What does your target audience need or want most? When you know what "it" is, make "it" the focus of your message.

You must assume that people don't care about you or your business. You must assume that your prospects are totally selfish. In all of your advertising, marketing, or selling, address only the benefits you are rendering the customer and prospect. It's all about them, not about you.

One of the most effective ways to relay the benefits to your prospects is through testimonials. People identify with other "real" people. In fact, some people are influenced more by testimonials than by any other part of your ad. The key point to remember is that the testimonials come from a believable, credible and likeable source. Effective testimonials touch your prospect's hot buttons. They sell by talking about the benefits you offer – the same benefits they, too, can enjoy.

Where do you get testimonials? There are basically two sources:

1. Unsolicited testimonials may come in a thank-you letter or call. Just get permission to use them in your promotions.

2. You can ask for testimonials in several ways. You can ask them in a letter, or even a customer satisfaction survey. Whatever works for you.

RULE #6: Close the sale.

Just as with personal selling, your advertisement must close the sale. Your ad needs to motivate the prospect to take immediate action. It needs to tell them exactly what to do: Order now, call us now, mail in this coupon now, come by our location today. Remember that the goal of direct response advertising is to get an immediate response from your offer. The response doesn't necessarily need to be an order; it can be to get your prospect to pre-qualify themselves so you can identify them.

There are several ways to induce a response with advertising. You can offer free reports, bonuses for responding immediately, discounts, coupons, and free estimates – anything that will prompt the prospect to action.

RULE #7: Always test your advertising.

Do you know what marketing leverage is? Marketing leverage is the reason why marketing is the single best investment any business has.

Here's a quick example. Let's say you're already running an ad that is generating 100 responses and 20 sales a week. Now let's say you try a new headline, and the number of responses increases to 120 a week. And what if you could raise the number of sales you get from those people responding (by using a different proposition, price, guarantee, etc.) from 20 to 36 sales per week. You have only increased each area by 20%, but look what happens to the big picture. That's 832 more sales in one year!

Now ask yourself this question: How much extra profit could you make for the same ad cost that you are spending right now? You must commit yourself to getting the best possible results from all of your advertising activities. Your market will tell you by their vote which headline, presentation, price, and guarantee they like best.

You can test the following parts of your advertising:

- Headlines
- Sales proposition

- Pricing
- Bonuses and incentives
- Guarantees and warranties
- One medium against another

How do you know which ones to use? You let your customers tell you what they like best. You don't have the right or the power to predetermine what your market wants.

But you do have the obligation to put every important marketing question to a vote by the only people that count - your prospects and customers. Remember this wonderful quote from one of the most recognized, respected, and influential entrepreneurs in American history:

"You don't build it for yourself. You ask the people what they want and then you build it for them."

- Walt Disney

Another benefit of testing is that you can test small and inexpensively. This way, when you decide to invest more money in an advertisement, you will be able to predict the results. You can test a couple of thousand prospects to see how a couple of million will respond.

There are different ways to test, but the important point to remember is to test only one variable at a time. This is the scientific principle of control. It means isolating the variables so you can be sure of the source of different results.

You should always analyze the results of the ads you run. This means you should code and track each sales concept you use. You want to know how each ad is performing – and how much it is costing. Without this data, you can't make good marketing decisions. How do you do it?

You can test by:

- Using coded coupons.

- Asking the prospect where they heard your message.

- Tell the prospect to specify a department number or person when they call or write.

- Use different telephone numbers for respondents.

- Use a code on a mailing label with an order form.

- Use different bonuses for different offers.

- Use different prices to see which one pulls the most prospects.

If you run two ads, and one pulls better than the other, try to figure out why. What actions did the two ads tell the reader to take? What words were used in the head-line? On what days did the ad appear, and on what page?

After you analyze which headline, offer and guarantee work best, try to improve on them. Test and retest one headline against another, one offer against another, one price against another, and so on.

Continually improving your advertising message will increase the efficiency of your advertising dollars and increase your profitability. Let the market tell you what it likes best about your ad. Guessing can be expensive.

How to Make Your Ads Stand Out

The majority of ads focus on one thing: Price. Just like many small businesses that compete on price, ads that compete on price usually don't pull very well. If they do pull well, you aren't making very much profit.

Come up with a different Unique Selling Proposition, one that doesn't focus on price. You need to have some strong reasons why customers should buy from you. Sell your ability to benefit the customer. This will make your ads stand out, and it will also build customer loyalty.

More guidelines to follow to make your ads more effective:

- Use subheadings between the headline and body-copy.

- Using a large initial letter in your body copy can increase readership by 13%.

- Use **serif type**. It is easier to read than **sans serif type.**

- Use bullets, asterisks, and numerical marks.

- **Emphasize** <u>important</u> *words*. Most people scan ads, use <u>underscore</u>, **bold** and *italics* to highlight important points of your message.

- When tested, long ads and copy pulled more sales than short ones.

- Use photographs that reinforce the selling message. Show what you are selling. This may sound simple, but over 50% of magazine ads have a photo of something other than what is being advertised.

- Use bonuses and incentives

- Get straight to the point

- Give the reader helpful advice

- Write in a language that everyone can understand

- Use captions

- Put the main benefit in the headline. Don't save the best for last.

- Specify right-hand page, outside column, as close to the front as possible - but don't pay extra.

- Indent your paragraphs

Things to avoid in your ads:

- If you have a lot of unrelated facts to present, don't try to relate them with cumbersome connectives; just number them or use bullets.

- Don't change your ads because you are tired of it. Your market will tell you when they are tired of it.

- Don't use type smaller than 9-point. It is difficult for many people to read. The copy in this newsletter is 10-point.

- Never set your copy in reverse (white type on black background).

- Don't say "I, Me, Mine, Us, or We." Do say "You and Your."

- Don't print in all CAPITAL LETTERS.

I hope the ideas I've shared with you prove to be helpful and inspiring. Your opportunity is to apply these concepts to your own advertisements to generate more sales and leads than ever before. Don't worry if other businesses in your industry don't advertise this way. Like I said earlier in this article, the vast majority of advertising is very ineffective. Follow the advice here and yours won't be.

How Many of the "Rules" Do You See in These Advertising Success Stories?

Using the same advertising tips and techniques mentioned in the article, I redesigned an advertisement for a dentist in Alexandria, VA.

First, we wrote a headline that captured the attention of his targeted audience. The headline read "How to Keep Your Teeth Until You're 90."

Next, we included useful and educational information in the ad that emphasized his area of expertise.

Finally, we offered a free report to anyone calling in and asking for it. The report was called, as you may have guessed, "How to Keep Your Teeth Until You're 90."

We ran the new ad in the same medium in which he ran his previous ad. Guess what? It immediately pulled 250% more responses.

The second success story I want to mention was with a golf club manufacturer. They had been running the same institutional-style ads in national and regional golf magazines for over a year. The ads were generating just enough sales to justify continuing to run the ad again. We applied several direct response advertising techniques to their advertisements:

1. Changed the headline to mention their main selling promise and their guarantee. The new headline read "The Straightest Golf Club You Have Ever Hit... 100% Guaranteed."

2. Added the subheading "If a team of rocket scientist were to design the perfect golf club, this would be it."

3. Packed the ad full of benefits to the reader.

4. Added pictures of the product to "show" the engineering advantages.

5. Added captions to explain the pictures.

6. Educated readers on why the golf club was superior.

7. Added testimonials from professional players.

8. Increased the guarantee form 30 days to a full year.

9. Added a bonus product that had a perceived value of $50, but a real cost of only $6.

10. And finally, we increased the price by 25%

The result of the first changes: sales increased by just under 300%.

But we didn't stop there. The next time the ad ran we swapped out the headline and subheading. This time the headline read "If a Team of Rocket Scientist Were to Design the Perfect Golf Club, This Would Be It."

The small change resulted in a 500% increase in sales over the original ad, and with 40% fewer returns.

Chapter 1 Notes

_____

_____

_____

_____

_____

_____

_____

_____

_____

_____

_____

_____

_____

_____

Chapter 2: How to Double Your Advertising Results

No question about it... advertising can be a headache. Sure, a good ad or mailing can bring in a hoard of new customers, but ads are expensive and inflexible, and postage rates continue to rise. And in the case of a Yellow Pages ad that doesn't work, it continues to cost you month in and month out for a full year. This report is packed with more information about print and mail advertising and how to make it deliver the customers and profits you want, than you're likely to find anywhere.

With no padding and few wasted words, it's packed with tips and techniques to make your cash register ring. Read it carefully and then use the techniques with every print ad you run. This year, when your ad representative comes around, don't say "Just rerun the same ad." Create an ad or mailing that captures attention and GETS RESULTS!

The Power of Advertising

The Yellow Pages can be a powerful advertising vehicle because of their long shelf life, and because it's advertising that almost every home gets. Most people expect to find certain types of businesses listed there, so they reach for the Yellow Pages as a primary source of information. They are the preferred choice of both a consumer and business buyer looking for products and services that aren't required on a regular basis. But here's what really makes the Yellow Pages such an effective marketing tool: People use them when they are ready to buy.

There are only two downsides to advertising in the directory. First, and largest, is the cost. Yellow Page ads are expensive. And the other negative factor is that you are advertising along with all your competitors at the same location. So you had better look good and your ad had better do well against the competition.

Most Yellow Page advertisers haven't a clue as to how to advertise in the directory, so the competitive ads are often a small consideration to the skillful advertiser. After you read this material, you will know more about Yellow Page advertising than 99.9% of your competitors.

If you're going to run any kind of advertising — print, mail or voice — you should do all you can to make it pay off. After all, it costs the same to run an ineffective ad, as it does to run a super-responsive one.

A quick look through the Yellow Pages directory or newspaper from any city reveals an abundance of weak, under-performing, look-a-like ads. Most of these advertisers are spending hundreds of dollars every month on ads that are totally unresponsive.

Here are 86 tips and tricks and an entire new advertising strategy that will in most cases double or triple the results of your advertising efforts. While some of the information pertains mainly to Yellow Pages advertising, much of it also applies to your other print or direct mail advertising.

1. Start Early

This one seems obvious, but it's the number one problem of all advertisers. Give yourself plenty of time to create your ad. Nothing breeds mediocrity like an impending deadline.

2. Know Your Deadlines

Know your deadlines in advance and beat them by a week or two. Once you've completed an ad, file it away for a day or two. When you look at it again, you'll likely come up with a few simple changes that will make your ad stronger. Don't be afraid to tinker with your ad until you've done all you can to improve response.

3. Plan Before You Start

Take some time to do a little planning before you start. The best ads have an outline or a framework to follow. Answer these questions:

- What results do you want to achieve?
- What approximate percentage of new business do you expect from your Yellow Pages ad?

- What action do you want to encourage prospects to take?

- Who is your target prospect?

- What is the biggest benefit you can offer in your ad?

- What are the secondary benefits that could also help draw responses?

- What approach will you use to capture attention and attract interest?

- What size of ad best meets your needs and budget?

- Which directories will your ad be placed in?

4. What are Your Competitors are Doing?

Then go in the opposite direction. Resist the temptation to present your advantages in the same way. You should definitely avoid the common approach used by most advertisers. That approach consists of:

- company name and logo

- brief description of products and/or services

- location and hours of operation

- something about what makes you special, or…

- company slogan

Since most advertisers use this basic format, or some similar variation, you should not. Distinction is the most important factor to consider and the greater your competition, the stronger your distinction needs to be. Your objective in creating any type of advertising should be to:

- Grab your prospect's attention.

- Sell this prospect on your unique advantages – advantages that distinguish you from everyone else in your field of endeavor.

- Encourage your prospect to take immediate action of some kind.

5. Get Inside Your Prospect's Mind

Visualize the mental process your prospect goes through when he needs the kind of product, service or solution you offer. Get inside your prospect's mind at the time he reaches for the Yellow Pages or reads your ad or mailing piece. This is the key to connecting with the people who ultimately determine your degree of success.

Put yourself in their shoes. Then ask yourself, "What would make me call one company over another?" Understanding the "wants" and "needs" of your market is a fundamental requirement of an ad that pulls superior results.

6. Research the Value of Color

Do a little research on your own before committing to colored ink. Additional colors (black is standard) cost more, so take the time to query advertisers who are currently using other colors. Ask if they've received more leads and/or customers, as a result of using additional color in their ads.

If your budget only allows for one option – additional colors OR a larger size ad – go with the larger display ad.

7. Consider Placement Options

Within each Yellow Pages directory there are often several different headings that may be suitable for your ad. A custom cabinetmaker may prefer an obvious category such as Cabinetmakers; however, potential clients might first search headings like Home Improvements or Woodworkers. You want to be sure to have an adequate presence wherever your prospects are most likely to look for your type of product or service. Choose the heading that's the best "fit" for your business.

8. Examine for Size

Look at each possible category and note the size of competing ads. If there are plenty of ads in a particular category, chances are that many of them are identical sizes.

Advertisers often have a tendency to do exactly as the competition does... Nothing more., nothing less. It seems reassuring on some level, but in fact it's a fatal flaw. **To succeed you need to stand apart from all** competitors instead of blending in. **Sameness breeds mediocrity.**

9. Check Ads Under Another Heading

Look at ads in a separate heading that's unrelated to your business. View the ads as a prospect would. Ask yourself: "Who would I call and why?"

Pay attention to your thought processes as you eliminate potential candidates from the running. Make a list of the things that made you favor one company over another. Do this for a few different headings and you'll gain some valuable insights into what elements attract business and what elements actually deter it.

10. Appeal to Customer Self-Interest

Ask yourself this question: "What is it that I'm really selling?" Rolex doesn't sell watches, they sell luxury. LensCrafters doesn't sell eyeglasses, they sell better eyesight. Seven-Eleven doesn't sell milk and bread, they sell convenience.

Take a closer look at your product or service. Find out the underlying reasons why people buy in your category. Then construct your ad to appeal to these important factors. Understanding why people buy is a prerequisite to creating an ad that works well.

11. The Essential Elements for a Profitable Ad

Create an outline of your ad using the 4 essential elements:

- Captivating Headline
- Unique Benefits
- Enticing Offer
- Contact Information

12. Check Other City Directories and Advertising Media

Study ads from other cities and other publications. You can find them at your local library or online. Look up your own specific category and observe how others have approached the same marketing challenges you're facing.

Browse through categories that are completely unrelated to your field. Keep your eyes open for ideas, concepts, strategies, or tactics that may be transferrable to your industry.

13. Decide on the Size of Your Ad Before You Begin the Design

Then create your ad to that exact size. Use whatever zoom function your software program features to make your ad the full size of your screen. This will help you make the smallest of adjustments quite easily and will prevent mistakes that are routinely overlooked at a scaled-down size.

14. Give Information

Give your prospects the information they need at the "moment of truth" when they're ready to make a purchasing decision.

Most Yellow Pages readers are ready to buy NOW. They only reach for the Yellow Pages and refer to a specific category when they are serious about finding a solution to a problem. They want to know who can best help them. Therefore, it stands to reason that your message should be based on solutions, advantages and customer benefits. Focus your message on what you do and how you benefit customers, rather than on who you are.

15. Create an Original Look

Design an ad that clearly and succinctly communicates your unique advantages and gives prospects a reason to call you. Your advertisement should answer a vital question: "What's special about your company and why should people call you?"

Take the time and make the effort to create an ad that works hard for you the whole year long. Focus on creating a distinctive, benefit-oriented ad.

16. Appeal to Their Wants

Use your most valuable space to attract interest by appealing to the "wants" of your customers. **The most common mistake and the biggest waste of prime advertising space is the use of a company name and/or logo at the top of the ad as a header.** To do this is to give up your most valuable space for something that is virtually meaning-less to your customers and prospects.

Choosing a display type ad frees you of the obligatory company name-heading format that other listings may require. Does your prospect really care what you've named your company? I highly doubt it.

What your prospect does care about is whether you have what he needs NOW. Can you provide the solution to his pressing problem?

17. Power of Size

Whatever space you can afford, put as much selling power in it as is absolutely possible. Many people equate advertising clout with success. For some, the bigger the ad, the more established... more impressive... more likely to meet the need a company appears.

This may be unfair, but it's also a reality. If you can't compete on size, compete on impact, power, and on motivating action.

18. Avoid Clichés

Stop using the same old tired, worn out clichés to describe your product or service. Phrases like "quality workmanship," "fast, reliable service," or "friendly staff" are too generic to be effective in attracting new customers.

Instead, **try to create something original, something that half a dozen other companies in the same category aren't also claiming to offer.**

19. Create a Distinctive Look and Feel

Sound-alike ads have a neutralizing effect on each other. Most ads in a given category basically say the same thing. They communicate the same message. One reason is that with a deadline fast approaching, the busy entrepreneur looks at the other ads in his specialty and creates his own based on what appears to be working for others. Big mistake.

20. Make Your Ad Look Different

Make your ad stand out head and shoulders above the rest of the ads on the page. This shouldn't be too difficult since 95% of all print ads follow the standard approach. Any departure from this traditional format is a step in the right direction.

Don't just look different, demonstrate your difference. How? By giving some information that is valuable at the time to the reader.

Remember, the reader is in a buying frame of mind. They are looking for solutions. And you can distinguish yourself by doing more than having an ad. Offer a solution to their problem, or more likely, offer a step in the direction of their solution.

For example, a safety supply house could offer a few safety tips; a mailing list broker could offer tips on how to test a list. This makes you unique because nobody else is doing this, giving you a decided advantage over your competition. In the next section you'll see a detailed example of how easily this can be done and how it makes your ad not only look different, but says a great deal about how you value and treat customers.

21. A Reason to Choose You

Make it clear to shoppers why they should choose you. Give them a strong reason. Offer an advantage. Spend most of your creative ad development on this. It's the most important part of your ad. **Present this information in your headline and follow it up quickly with a few bullet-point reasons for your prospects to call or visit you.**

22. How to Have a Distinctive Ad

Establish distinction three ways:

1. the layout

2. the verbal description

3. the overall visual design of your ad.

The process should begin with a review of competing ads.

For example, consider using plenty of words detailing your advantages if your competitors use just a handful.

Try a poster-like announcement that stands out like a beacon when surrounded by the sameness of typical ads.

23. Be Novel

Venture out into new territory. A riveting, never-seen-before ad can have a lasting effect on those exposed to it and a very profitable effect on you.

Powerful communications can leave an indelible impression on the minds of shoppers who may be candidates for your product or service in the future. Memorable ads have impact long after the directory has been placed back on the shelf. Beat others to the punch and reap the rewards before they can copy your style.

24. Fear and Hope

Use human nature to your advantage. The two levers of human motivation are the fear of loss and the hope for reward. All buying motivations boil down to one of the two. A solid knowledge of your prospect should lead you to the most effective approach for your audience. Using this strategy can be strikingly powerful when appropriately applied.

25. Dare to Be Different

After all, it's your business. It's your future and the future of all those who depend on you. You're the one who invested the capital. You take the risks. So never settle for an ad that looks the same as all the others.

To rise above the competition, cast your company in a different light. Never settle for average results. This is apparently what most advertisers want – the same kind of results as their competitors are getting. It may be enough to get by. You could even do quite well. But any similarity to your competitors' ads will only weaken your own results.

Avoid the mold set by others. Instead, strive for differentiation. If you want to achieve breakthrough results, you have to be willing to break with tradition.

26. Reward Them

Make people feel good about their decision to call you. Reward them. Welcome them. Over-deliver on the promises mentioned in your ad. That's a sure way of generating repeat business.

Remember, a prospect that calls based on your ad, has certain preconceived notions about your company. You are held in high regard, at least for the moment. Your prospect has high hopes and expectations. You have a standard to live up to beginning with the way the call is answered.

27. An Ad is Part of Your Marketing Mix

Use the Yellow Pages, display and direct mail advertising in conjunction with other advertising and marketing methods.

Marketing includes everything you do to promote your business from the moment you conceive it, to the service you provide after the sale.

Multiple media equals multiplied exposure. A marketing mix that involves several methods of promotion is more effective than any single method.

28. Maintain a Single Focus

Most consumers tend to remember one thing only from any given advertisement, if they remember anything at all. For this reason, I recommend using one strong claim in your headline and then following along this theme with additional facts presented as benefits to substantiate this central claim. Beware of competing facts that may dilute your message.

29. Offer a Solution

Present what you offer as an immediate solution to a problem... an answer to a need... the gratification of a desire. Remember that Yellow Pages shoppers are ready to buy so give them what they want, when they want it.

30. Use Enhancements

Boost the power of your ad by using proven enhancements. Components that can make your Yellow Pages ad stronger include:

- USP (Unique Selling Proposition) – an original, identifiable claim that separates you from all competitors.

- Premiums -Freebies or incentives to encourage response.

- Credibility Boosters – proof that you have what it takes to best supply what buyers want.

- Features connected to benefits – adds power, believability and understanding to any benefits offered.

31. Don't Find You In the Yellow Pages

Avoid telling prospects that they can "find you fast in the Yellow Pages." This is a terrible mistake – yet it's being made all the time. Sure, your prospective customers might find you there, but they'll also find your competitors. This eliminates any advantage you might have had. There are plenty of other ads vying for the same prospect's attention and business.

32. Track All Responses

Knowing where the call originated is critical in determining future advertising strategy. When you have the same ad running in multiple directories, it pays to know which directory a caller used to locate you.

Sometimes it may be obvious. Other calls won't be as easy to trace back to a specific listing. Identifying the source of every caller gives you an accurate measurement of each ad's effectiveness.

33. Sell the Sizzle

The Yellow Pages is a dictionary-like resource guide used by huge numbers of ready-to-buy shoppers. Many reach for the Yellow Pages because they need information. They want the facts, so give them facts. But provide it with a little sizzle. When you stress the benefits you're selling the sizzle. Your challenge is to make your benefits more appealing than your competitors.

34. Test and Record

Test and record the effectiveness of each ad. This provides you with valuable data you can use to choose the size and placement of future ads. The easiest way to measure your ad's results is to list a separate telephone number for each ad -one that isn't advertised or used for any other purpose. When the phone rings, you'll automatically be able to identify the advertisement that triggered it.

35. An Additional Phone Line

Provide a secondary phone line where prospects call for detailed information, product updates, special sell-offs or discounted prices. This number should play a lesser role visually in the ad, apart from the main telephone number you want prospects to use.

Having a separate number allows interested prospects to gather additional information anonymously. It gives you the opportunity to sell more products or services using voice mail as the medium.

36. Protect Your Ad

Protect yourself from having your winning ad stolen by a competitor. When you've employed some of these concepts and you have an ad that looks like a sure-fire success, add a brief copyright notice.

Simply place the following somewhere in your ad in small type: copyright ©2001 (your company name). This kind of notice serves as a deterrent, one that should make would be thieves think twice before attempting to rip-off your winning ideas.

37. Details You Need

Supply the details Yellow Pages shoppers want to see. Here's a list of some of the things typical buyers want and look for:

- Fast service
- Reputable companies
- Availability
- Professionalism
- Guarantees

- Free offers

- Specialization

- Specific numbers

- Hours of business

- Location

- Why they should choose you

- Reliability

- Capability

- Easy access

38. A Headline That Attracts

Write an attention-getting headline that appeals to the market you want to reach. The headline is the most important component of an ad. The headline is the lure that instantly communicates your primary advantages over all others.

A strong benefit-oriented headline is critical to achieving maximum results from your ad. Lead with a headline instead of your company name.

39. A Reason to Respond

Give your audience a reason to respond to your ad. Provide a call to action. Invite them to call or visit for a free sample or premium. You can build your own in-house list of prospects this way, a list you can later mine, over and over again. These are qualified prospects for the kind of products/services that you offer, by virtue of the fact they took the time to reply.

40. Offer Tips

Position yourself as helpful and interested in serving the needs of your market. Separate your business from all others by offering a few simple tips in your area of expertise that could save people time, money, or spare them frustration and aggravation.

For example, a safety supply house could offer a few safety tips; an ailing list broker could offer tips on how to test a list. The information could be presented in a side bar of your ad. Information presented in this manner produces a visual draw, without detracting from your sales message.

This strategy gives you a decided advantage over your competition. When help of a related kind is required, you have a greater chance at being the business of choice.

Offering a few helpful ideas benefits you in 4 ways:

- It makes your ad different from the others.
- It creates warm feelings towards your company.
- It helps place you in the category of an expert.
- It makes you unique. Nobody else is doing this.

41. Add Headline Power

Pack extra punch into your headline. **With a smaller ad you won't be able to put in many**

details, so the headline is even more important. It's your strongest lure. That's why the company name as a headline just doesn't cut it.

A smaller ad with impact will out-pull a larger ad without it. The key to implementing impact is to hit quickly and hit hard with your most powerful benefit message. How? One way is to use an over-sized, bold headline that gets right to the point. Your headline must attract the attention of your prospect by appealing to his/her specific wants, needs or desires. Then follow up with several quick, bullet-point benefits that can be read at a glance. Impact makes the difference.

42. Create a Different Message

Create a different message and present it with your own flair. Find your strongest, most appealing advantage, then, present it in a way that beckons the reader's attention. Be original. All the other ads on the pages are shouting out to the same prospects, trying to grab their attention. For your ad to reach out and grab the prospect, it must be unique amidst the sea of similarities. One way to do this is with a short headline in large type, draped diagonally across the ad space.

43. Stop the Reader

Arrest the attention of your prospect. Stop him cold. The most effective headlines are stoppers; they immediately halt the reader in his tracks and pull him in to read the rest of your ad. Even the scanning eye is magnetically drawn inside by the irresistible pull of a good headline.

44. Short Headlines

Keep your headlines short and to the point. I recommend using no more than a handful of words... up to seven or eight, maximum. If you can generate the right kind of attention with fewer words, all the better.

45. Benefits... Not Features

Stress the benefits, not the features. Features are the physical characteristics of your product or service. The benefits are the useful or helpful advantages provided by a feature. The benefits are what the customer gets as a result of owning the product. Benefits are the reasons why most people buy.

46. Add Personality

Add some personality to your advertising. Show your prospects that behind your business name are sincere people who genuinely care about those they serve.

Make your ad communicate on a personal level. Projecting an image of your company as one of concern could be as simple as mentioning the local charity to which you contribute regularly. Infusing your ads with a personal touch separates you from the companies who seem only interested in lining their own pockets.

47. Be Clear and "To the Point"

Be clear, concise, informative and persuasive. Avoid industry jargon and product names that are not well known and instantly recognizable to your audience. Avoid common statements that are so overused they don't mean anything anymore. Like "best service in town."

48. Inform

Include lots of information. The more you tell, the more you sell. Don't waste valuable space. Provide every conceivable benefit, every reason you can give for doing business with your company. Provide more relevant information than your competitors.

49. Selling Words

Use words that sell the prospect on doing business with you. Avoid flat, bland advertising that generates a ho-hum response. **Everything about your ad should be geared toward generating action.** It's this action that leads to more immediate sales or sets the sales process in motion.

50. Say It Differently

Phrase your benefits in a unique way that's markedly different from the competition. Make them more compelling and more impressive. Don't just say the identical thing your competitor does. A quick glance through any Yellow Pages directory will show you how many businesses say basically the same things as their competitors.

51. Know Your Audience

Instill a sense of empathy and understanding for you target market. In order to do this, you have to first have an accurate knowledge of your audience's "wants" and "needs." Talk to your current customers. Find out why they reward you with their business.

52. Use Testimonials

Boost your ad's power with a strong testimonial headline. It works better in some categories than others, particularly those where prospective customers may have a fear of being ripped off.

One example is the home service or renovations industry. This would include plumbers, roofers, general contractors, painters, etc. "ABC Plumbing came To the Rescue, At A Price No One Else Could Touch."

Follow up a testimonial with a list of why a prospect should choose your service over another.

53. Give Directions

Direct your prospects to you. Make it easy for them to reach you. Depending on your type of business and location, you may want to display a map as well as a listing of your hours of business.

In some situations it may be preferable to provide a directional line such as "next to Union Station on Front Street," rather than a map. Make the information available that would allow any reader to reach you on the first try, whether by visiting or calling.

54. Build Credibility

Consider credibility-builders such as significant customers that have used your service, the number of years you've been in business, your industry experience or any unusual recognition you may have received.

Uniqueness stands out. (I know we said that the number of years in business doesn't belong in most ads, but if it is unusually long, then it could help support your credibility). But it's not a benefit!

55. Sell with Specifics

Specific details are more believable than vague generalities. A seminar company claiming to have delivered a "Computer Care Maintenance Course to 4,719 students in 2000," has a higher degree of realism that the firm that says "thousands attended our programs in 2000."

56. Give Answers

Increase your chances of getting calls from your ads by providing the important answers that prospects seek.

Yellow Pages shoppers usually know what they want and they're ready to buy when they call. Often the only remaining decision to be made is where to buy. You can make that decision easier on the prospect by providing relevant details of importance.

People want to know that you have the answer to their problem. And they want to know that you can be trusted. Give them the proof they need to call you first.

57. Importance of Ad Layout

Command attention to your ad with an attractive layout. Here are 3 qualities of a good ad layout that attracts attention and produces results:

- Visually appealing and easy-to-look-at presentation.

- Conveys a feeling of action.

- Avoids perfect balance and symmetry, the "sameness" that only helps an ad blend in, rather than stand out.

58. Bullets and Lists

Highlight the elements that make your company, product line, or services, different and special. You can do this in your supporting copy. Bullet points and numbered lists help to keep these details organized and hard-hitting.

Use bullet points or numbered lists to communicate your best benefits in a concise, succinct and organized manner.

This kind of point-form presentation can improve efficiency in how your information is relayed to the reader. Short, powerful, bite-size chunks of information allow you to present your most vital benefits or product details, quickly.

59. Make Your Number Visible

Make it easy for the reader to locate and read your contact information. Most people respond to Yellow Pages ads by phone. After all, it is a phone book. Therefore, it seems logical that the primary contact information should be your telephone number. Make it visually prominent. Big, bold and clear for all to see.

Place your telephone number at the bottom of your ad. It should be the natural conclusion to your message -the point to which you ultimately direct your prospect.

60. Use Reverses

Draw the eye with a "reverse -type" format. Reverse-type (white letters on a black background) can be a useful attention grabber when used correctly. A little goes a long way. Highlight one or two areas of your ad, at most. Over-use nullifies its impact.

The human eye is naturally drawn to any dark objects on the page, first. Try it for headlines, special offers, telephone numbers, or testimonials.

It's a great place to add an extra push by listing a strong extra benefit that your competition either doesn't offer, or doesn't promote. For example, a firewood supplier would likely offer a delivery service as part of regular operations. Some may offer it free, others for a slight additional charge. But an intelligent startup company could offer free stacking for seniors. This is a unique benefit, worthy of drawing extra attention via reverse-type.

61. Keep It Clean

Maintain as clean a look as possible, while still delivering impact. Ads that are cluttered with too much information in too small an area are less effective than those that jump right out at you and are easy to read.

62. Payment Methods

Let people know how you do business. Display any credit cards that you accept. Indicate all acceptable forms of payment, other than cash. Don't give the anxious buyer a reason to go somewhere else instead. Tell all about the convenience you offer.

63. First Impressions

Make a strong first impression. The overall visual presentation can cause prospects to make an instant decision as to how they feel about you and whether yours is a business they want to connect with. Create an ad that projects a good, positive feeling, vibration or impression.

64. Selling Space

Allow adequate space in your ad so your most prominent, prospect-centered points really stand out. Get the largest ad you can afford. Avoid over-crowding and cramming. Surrounding a block of text with a little space draws attention to those featured words. It catches attention and appears to be a less formidable task to wade through. In effect, you are "framing" your text, signaling its importance, which in turn motivates readership.

65. Importance of Ad Layout

Multiply the effectiveness of your graphics with "captions." Captions are those words attached to photographs, cartoons or other visuals. A strong graphic with a caption has the power to command more attention than the graphic ever could on its own.

Captions that provide important benefit details in a few words can have significant effects on results. **Captions are one of the most-read components on an ad.** Why? Human nature. Analyzing a graphic requires thinking. The natural tendency is to read the caption to get a quick understanding of the whole picture.

Since a caption attracts a large readership you can improve your ad's results by filling it with hard-hitting, benefit-oriented sales copy.

66. Use of Call Outs

Complement a graphic with a "call-out." The call-out is simply a line that leads from one element of a graphic to a textual definition or description.

The advantage of the call-out is that, even when the reader knows what is being singled out, they can't help but be drawn to the verbal description. Use this to your advantage by giving the reader another strong reason to patronize your business over another.

67. Use Balloons

Command the attention of your prospects with a "balloon." Balloons work the same way as call-outs and captions as attention-getting devices. Balloons are the circled words found in comic strips or photos that indicate the thoughts or feelings of the subject.

The appearance of a balloon signals to the reader the location of necessary details. It's no surprise that they rank very high in terms of must-read ad copy.

68. Attention. Interest. Desire. Action.

Your entire ad must be easy to follow with all elements working together to produce a coherent message. Start with your headline and conclude with your phone number and a call to action such as "CALL NOW for your FREE ESTIMATE!"

69. One Dominant Feature

Make one single element the dominant visual feature. A bold headline or a striking graphic that instantly communicates your message is the most important part of your ad. It should stand out as the one eye-catching element that reaches out and nudges the eyeballs of the prospect. An attention-arresting visual is the tool that ensures the rest of the ad gets a reading.

70. Frame With Space

Use your available space to effectively communicate your marketing message. To make sure your message gets across, it must be easy to read and understand. "White space" can be an important ally. The correct use of spacing provides a rest for the eye. It also helps set off the important points by framing them, making them appear more significant.

71. Be Out of Place

Do the unexpected. Research indicates that typically the human eye reacts in a certain way. Normally, the eye goes from dark areas to lighter areas, from large objects to small, from brighter areas to dimmer ones. The eye focuses on things that appear out of place. This could involve shapes, colors, sizes and the positioning of elements within the ad. Use this valuable data to make the readers eyes go where you want them to go.

72. Insist Upon Legibility

Avoid type that is less than ten points in size. You don't want to cause any strain for your reader. In fact, you want to make it incredibly easy for them to get the information. Also be careful with script fonts or other fancy fonts that may look good to you. Font selection is not the place to let your creative mind soar. This choice should be based on clarity, readability and overall appearance. Stick to one font throughout, or, one headline font with a compatible, separate font for the body copy. Limit your type sizes to three different variations.

73. Avoid Tints

Avoid placing copy on tints or shaded areas. It's more difficult to read and therefore, easier to avoid. Clarity of communication should be given primary consideration throughout the ad design process.

74. Grab Attention

Focus your design efforts on immediately capturing your prospect's attention. The most effective ads work almost instantaneously. As soon as the page is turned, this ad jumps right out at you, demanding your focus. To maximize your ads potential it must work at-a-glance.

75. Follow Visual Appeal Rules

Capitalize on natural visual appeal. Headlines and illustrations are always seen first, before typical body copy. These elements need to work as the pull that brings the reader into the heart of the message.

76. Use Emphasis Tools

Take advantage of the availability of "tools of emphasis." Bullet-points, numbers, bold lettering, boxes of various shapes and sizes, checklists, asterisks, underlining, etc., can all be used effectively to emphasize key words. Don't use them all... choose a maximum of three tools in any given ad. And, don't try to emphasize everything to the same degree. To emphasize everything is to emphasize nothing.

77. Color Rules

Consider colors carefully. Color can make your ad stand out. Color naturally draws the eye if the ads around you are all black. Studies show that color can boost readership, improve retention and even increase a buyer's tendency to purchase. However, keep these points in mind...

1. You are usually limited to a few stock colors only. (Usually red, green, blue and white)

2. Your background remains a constant yellow – not the most compatible background shade.

3. If your colored ad appears on a page with several other colored ads, any eye-catching appeal has been lost altogether.

78. Select a Different Format

Select a format that is different from the competition. Consider unusual approaches like an editorial style that simulates a public service announcement, or, a letter format, from one individual to another. A copy-rich design can draw attention when all the ads around it use small amounts of brief, point-form text. (Read the next section for complete details of the benefits of this approach with examples.)

79. What Stays and What to Delete

Utilize every element that assists with the sales message and delete any that doesn't. Avoid unnecessary artwork that doesn't contribute to the sales message. Artwork shouldn't be used as decoration. If it doesn't help sell, it doesn't belong.

80. What to Stress

Make your telephone number stand out. The most important contact information in an ad is usually the telephone number. Make it a prominent part of your ad. Also consider including other important contact details like:

- Street address
- Fax number
- Web address
- E-mail address

For retailers, providing a street address is essential. For a consultant working from home a phone number alone would likely be the preferred contact listing.

81. Name Value

Feature your name prominently, if your firm is well known in the marketplace. If you're a relative unknown vying for the reader's attention, you probably shouldn't make a big deal out of your name. It takes years to develop name recognition. If you've got it, use it.

82. Secret of Benefiting From Attention-Getting Devices

Lead towards a competitive advantage with any attention-getting device used. If you're going to use shadow boxes, starbursts, reverse-type, etc., use them to highlight your major selling points like testimonials, headlines, free offers, or major benefits.

In the Yellow Pages you're surrounded by the competition. On a page filled with competing ads, you want to direct your prospect's attention to your big advantage — something you offer that others don't.

83. Use Border or Frame

Use the border or frame that outlines your ad to attract interest. Again, the key is creating a standout border that is unique, and visually magnetic.

Consider all options including: thicker lines, rounded corners, dotted lines or original artwork as a border. But don't make it so detailed that it detracts from your message. You want to create an ad that is the dominant one on the page or under a given heading but still reflects good taste and favorably upon the business.

84. When to Use Photos

Insert photographs when they help to convey the image, tone, or feeling of your business. A photo of yourself can be particularly advantageous when you're selling intangibles like personal counseling, financial planning or life insurance.

In this kind of selling situation, you're really selling yourself. People feel reassured when they can see what you look like. They feel more comfortable... it's almost as if they've already met you.

Be certain that your self-portrait is a quality shot and that you "look" the part for the role you play in your business. You want to be sure you convey the right image.

85. Don't Overuse Design Elements

Utilize simple design options like boxes, drop shadows, pull quotes, arrow starbursts bold, italicized or underlined text. Employ these enhancements with care. Avoid overuse. Using too many of these devices in a single ad will only create a scrambled, unprofessional look.

86. Use of Copy Blocks

Focus your prospect's attention by using solid blocks of black or another color option. Type placed on a solid block stands out visually and is easier to read than text placed on blends or shaded colors. Whenever you're using reverse-type, always use solid blocks of dark colors.

Conclusion

As you've discovered throughout this report, there are many mistakes business owners and executives are making with their sales and marketing efforts. The good news is that with an intelligent and systematic approach toward growing your business, you can create an unstoppable marketing machine with many powerful competitive advantages within your marketplace.

Chapter 2 Notes

_____

_____

_____

_____

_____

_____

_____

_____

_____

_____

_____

_____

_____

Chapter 3: Smart Marketing Checklist

How to Never Make Another Bad Marketing Decision Ever Again.

Marketing is (or at least it should be) an investment in your business. In fact, it is one of only two functions in your business that makes you money. Consider this quote from one of the most influential business minds of the 20th Century:

"Because its purpose is to create a customer, a business has only two functions: marketing and innovation. Marketing and innovation produce results, everything else is a cost."

- Peter Drucker

A Guide to Assist You in Marketing Decisions

This chapter is intended to serve as a guide to help you make smart marketing decisions. Used properly marketing will produce returns in the form of increased sales, new customers, and greater profits. It can help you achieve competitive advantages in your marketplace.

But the unfortunate truth is that most marketing fails. And there's a real cost associated with that failure: your marketing dollars.

But I want to help you change all that, and that's why I created this report. Use it to assist in making wise marketing decisions in the following areas:

1. To help you effectively choose media and advertising opportunities.

2. Serve as a guideline in the creation of advertisements and marketing pieces that produce results.

3. Assist you in scrutinizing advertising and marketing agencies, consultants, or other professionals you are considering working with.

And we get started with this on the next page.

What Do You Want To Achieve?

This may seem obvious, but for your marketing to be successful you must know two things:

- You must understand what you want to accomplish and what success will look like.

- You must have a means of measuring your results.

Functions of Marketing – Here are 10 legitimate objectives that marketing can accomplish. It's up to you to decide which functions are most important, and what marketing tools you need to use to achieve them.

1. **Lead Generation** – this is the creation of prospective customers for your business. All businesses must have leads, and there are many methods you can use to get them.

2. **Education** of your target market and ideal customers about your product or service. Depending on the complexity of your product or service, pricing, and other market conditions, some businesses must spend considerable amount of time and money on this function of marketing.

3. **Conversion** of prospects into customers, also known as "closing" the deal.

4. **Word of Mouth and Referrals** – Every business loves referrals, so why not get proactive in generating more referrals.

5. **Increase the Average Transaction Value** – This is simply getting your customers and clients to spend more money each time they purchase from you.

6. **Increase Customer Purchase Frequency** – This is getting your customers to purchase from you more often, and to stay with you for a longer period of time.

7. **Improve Customer Loyalty** – This one can be difficult to measure, but being considered unique and frequently communicating value to your customers is the easiest means of improving customer loyalty.

8. **Reduce Customer Attrition or Turnover** – The average business loses 20% - 40% of their customers on a yearly basis (this is called attrition), and businesses that don't market to their current customer base can lose up to 50% of their customers each year. That's a complete turnover of a customer base every 2– 5 years.

9. **Reactivate Inactive Customers** – This is when you make an effort to reclaim your lost customers and get them to start doing business with you again.

10. **Market Research** – to collect relevant data about your customers, prospects and market conditions. The key is to understand what data is relevant to your marketing and business success.

Smart Marketing Checklist

Now that you understand what the marketing functions are, it's time to get to scrutinize your marketing activity. Use the checklist below to help you decide if the activity has a good chance of being an investment in growing your business.

Questions to answer either "yes" or "no."

1. Will this marketing effort effectively reach your target market and ideal customers? If it doesn't, stop now… it's a waste of your money.

2. Will the marketing effort properly motivate your prospects to allow you to achieve your Desired Response or Action?

3. Will you be able to track and measure the results of the marketing activity so you can hold it accountable for results?

4. Will your advertisement or marketing piece stand out from others, or will it be lost among many other ads in the same media?

5. Does running this ad or marketing effort provide you with any competitive advantages? If so, what are they?

6. Is the media you're considering consistent with your image and message?

7. Will the marketing activity help generate Word of Mouth or Referrals business? How?

8. Does the marketing effort assist you in improving customer loyalty? If so, how does it do that?

9. Will your advertisement fly underneath your prospect's "advertising radar", or will it look just like every other ad of your competitors?

10. Is the main goal of your marketing effort to increase awareness or build your brand? If so, stop! Make sure brand building is a secondary objective, not the primary focus of your marketing.

11. If your marketing effort fails, what will the media or agency do to reimburse or compensate you for your lost money?

Notes

Chapter 4: Make the Internet Work for Your Business

How to use the world's most powerful media to increase Sales and lower marketing costs

The Ugly Truth

Numerous recent market tests and surveys prove an increasing number of buyers are going to the internet and search engines to locate merchants they will shop with. Over the last 10 years this trend has increased steadily and is now hitting full stride with local businesses.

I created this special report with two main objectives in mind:

1. Explain how local businesses can use the web to grow in sales, profits, and market share.

2. Address what I call the "Ugly Truth" about websites and internet marketing: There are over 120 million active websites on the internet, and most accomplish nothing. Yours doesn't have to be one of them.

How the Internet is Changing Business

In the early days, the internet was generally thought to be a means of connecting people from around the world to share data, information, and to improve communication. These things soon became second nature, and big business recognized the flexibility and power of this new media and began taking it to an entirely new level. Soon every major corporation had an online presence, and even the most traditional businesses were forced to embrace this technology.

In 2000, many large corporations and highly capitalized start-ups spent millions of dollars on both online and offline advertising attempting to drive people to their respective websites. This proved not to be a viable business model because the internet simply wasn't mature enough to accommodate such huge spending. Suddenly everything fell apart, and in the wake of the "dot com crash", it seemed that even big businesses were going to struggle on the internet.

However, over the last few years things have changed dramatically. Technology has improved, tens of millions of people are surfing the web daily, and the internet is now a trillion-dollar industry.

We are now much better prepared to harness the true power of the internet, and a new internet generation is beginning to flourish: the local small business.

This chapter is a closer look at why the internet is such a powerful tool for local business, and how you can take advantage of this new media and technology for the growth of your business.

A Big Shift in Advertising

Offline:

- Print yellow pages and directories
- Newspapers
- Radio
- Television

Online:

- Search engine marketing
- Email marketing
- Social media marketing

Small business owners, executives and entrepreneurs are continually searching for marketing activities that produce real and measureable results in sales, profits and market share. Although this quest has always been challenging, over the past few years it has become even more complicated and frustrating.

Small business has been hit hardest by the economic recession, with many reporting sales down more than 30%. Not only that, but marketing activities that used to work for them (yellow pages, newspaper, radio, television, print ads, etc.) are no longer producing the same results… and they're getting even more expensive.

The Big Advertising Shift

Ask almost any business owner and they'll tell you that they know the internet is the future, but they don't know how to capitalize on it. You can't blame them… There's so much bad information out there about marketing on the internet that it's nearly impossible to know what to believe. Worse than that, many of you have already invested in expensive websites or internet marketing programs that don't do anything to accomplish your business goals.

Don't become jaded or close-minded just yet, because the internet does offer incredible opportunity to local business owners who use it properly, and that's what this report is about.

Incredible Opportunity for Local Small Business

The internet is the fastest growing and largest medium of information in history. In fact, it's larger than newspapers, radio and television combined. Additionally, there are more internet users worldwide than users of all other mediums combined.

There's no arguing over the size and reach of the internet, but to fully understand its potential for local small business, take a look at the follow data:

- 70 % of US households use the internet for research when shopping locally for products and services (The Kelsey Group).

- 31% of all business-to-business buyers turn to a search engine first when looking for local products and services (NPD Group).

- Product research and comparison shopping happens online, but 67% of those purchases happen offline (Accenture).

- 73% of online activity is related to local content (Google).

- For every dollar US consumers spend online, they spend five or six on offline purchases influenced by online research (MIT Technology Review).

Many entrepreneurs and executives operating at a local level have been slow and reluctant to embrace the internet as a viable media for their businesses. But the truth is that there are tons of local buyers looking for your products and services, and the internet is the best way for them to find you.

Maybe you've noticed that local and regional search engines and directory sites are becoming much more visible. This is because the major search engines are giving them higher ranking in search results. This is not a fad; it's a very visible trend. Every day more and more of your customers are looking for you online. Don't make the mistake of ignoring these trends or your customers.

Consider the following local search data:

- 43% of all Google searches include a geographical identifier (Google).

- 84% of US internet users perform regular local searches. That's 129 million people (DM News).

Here's an important question you need to ask yourself: Can your customers and prospects find you online, or are they finding your competitors? Unless you are easily found on the internet, you are losing both current and future customers and clients. Having an effective online presence is very important to the growth of your business.

Online Marketing That Works for Local Business

It's no secret that the landscape of the local internet changes constantly. There are new methods of promotion discovered every month. Search engines change their algorithms frequently, and rankings can change daily.

The strategies that I use and recommend have worked for years, and they will continue working for many more. There is a ton of information available about marketing on the internet. The problem comes when trying to figure out what really works... and what is just a waste of time and money.

This chapter is for local business owners, managers, and entrepreneurs that want the internet to make them money. And to get results from your internet marketing efforts you must have local internet marketing experience and expertise.

The internet marketing process that I use for clients is the same one I've used with several of my own businesses to achieve the following results:

- Create, launch and manage a web-based alliance of 50 businesses all marketing to Atlanta homeowners. This online alliance became the most profitable marketing initiative for over 30 of our partners.

- Created a website and online club with the purpose of helping investors buy and sell real estate in Atlanta. This website became the most highly visited local real estate website averaging over 300 unique visitors daily. The club and website assisted in selling almost 200 investment properties valued at over $27,000,000.

- Launched a home renovations website with the purpose of generating leads for local Atlanta contractors. The company website was able to achieve first page rankings in Google in less than two weeks, and ranked first for the competitive search terms of "Atlanta home renovations" and "Atlanta home remodeling."

I'm not writing this to boast; just to lend credibility to my simple online marketing process. As you can see by the examples above, this process can drive revenues to many different local business models.

Online marketing is not difficult to do, but it's not easy to learn. There is so much bad information out there, and it can be difficult separating the good from the bad. So unless you have months to spend learning and testing your online marketing efforts, it can be a very frustrating experience.

Maybe you've tried online marketing activities in the past and failed. If that's the case, it's unfortunate... but you're the norm, not the exception.

Driving Offline Sales with Online Marketing

As a local business owner or manager, you have probably been marketing yourself and your business to the local community through traditional means such as word of mouth, radio, television, newspapers, yellow pages, conventions, trade shows, and charity events. While taking your business online can be exciting, there are many ways you can get stuck spinning your tires, never gaining real traction or momentum.

Your core business probably won't change when you market online. The internet can be an extremely effective media for reaching prospects and customers, but your primary goal remains the same... and that is to drive people to your business. After all, it's still an offline business, and you must physically connect with your customers.

Marketing your business online is simply positioning your website and marketing messages in front of your target market when they are researching the products and services you provide… and most importantly, compelling them to take action.

Many business owners don't even realize that there are potential clients and customers using the internet every week trying to find them.

Chances are, there are hundreds, if not thousands, of local people looking for your products and services each month. Later on in this report I'm going to show you a simple way to discover for yourself the potential in building a direct response website and what a strong online presence can do for you.

A Mistake Too Many Business Owners Make

It's important for you to understand that marketing a website is completely different than creating a website.

Many small business owners have friends or family create their websites, or they look for the least expensive option possible just so they can get a website online. They're hesitant to spend $3,000 for a good direct response website, so their conversion rates suffer. The truth is, they probably could double their call-to-action rates (they call you, email you, fill out a form, etc.) on their sites with just a small investment.

Most often these websites are created by someone that has a graphic design or "techie" background. Remember, the purpose of the website is marketing. You wouldn't hire a carpenter to sell your house, and you shouldn't hire a graphic artist or techie to market your website.

It's very rare that any one person has all of the critical skills needed to create and effectively market a website, so be careful when choosing a personal friend or low-cost option. If you do, your conversion will suffer.

Your website is a marketing endeavor, and it's important that you treat it like one. The goal is to maximize conversion, so the design and marketing of your website is an absolutely critical component… Don't skimp or settle on this .

Driving Website Traffic and Conversion

There are dozens of ways to drive traffic to your website, but in this report I'm only going to cover a few proven strategies and tactics that consistently work very well. I've specifically chosen these because they drive the most amount of traffic that takes action, or converts. In local business internet marketing, quality traffic that converts is what counts.

Your business website needs to engage visitors and get them to interact with your company...

Enter Web 2.0. Maybe you've heard of it? Web 2.0 is all about interaction, and the good news here is that 99% of your competitors still have Web 1.0 websites... More on this later.

Interactive goals for your website can include capturing leads, getting visitors to join your mailing/email list, filling out a form, participating in a survey, posting on your forum, joining your social network, or just picking up the phone and calling. Most websites are just online brochures with no interactive functions.

Your website must be designed to not only maximize the calls-to-action, but also maximize the number of visitors who interact with your site.

Local Business Websites That Work

A company website showcasing your business, products and services is a likely first step in creating your online presence. All you need is a simple website providing clear information about the products or services you provide. There's no need to stuff your website with pages and pages about your industry; your target market doesn't care about that. They only care about their immediate needs, so it's important that the content on your website answers any questions they may have about your products, services, and the buying process.

Your website needs to show prospective customers your business can be trusted, and the best way to do that is through engaging copy focusing on the benefits your customers receive from you. One of the biggest sins in marketing is to be boring. Visitors to your website will quickly leave if they are inundated with uninteresting history and copy that is all about you, and not about them.

Even big businesses that are historically formal and stuffy have recognized they can't be overly serious in their online presence. They now understand it's imperative to appeal to many different audiences, so they've created more diverse websites that speak in a more informal tone, assisting in building rapport and trust.

The Branding Website or Online Brochure: All Looks... No Brains

Many business owners have had expensive websites built with hopes of it becoming a great investment in the growth of their business. Unfortunately for the overwhelming majority, those hopes never materialize.

I define a branding website as an online brochure that accomplishes very little. They may be very pretty to look at, but lack any real marketing substance. They don't promote visitor interaction, and they don't have strong calls-to-action.

Branding websites are a waste of time and money.

Again, they are often built by friends, techies, and graphic designers (sometimes very talented ones)… but they lack solid online direct response marketing principles.

Because these sites don't have a solid marketing foundation, often search engines never list them and visitors rarely interact with them. If visitors aren't interacting with your website, you're losing out. Even worse, if your competitors are drawing customers away from you with high performing websites, then you're losing out even more.

The good news is that if you're the owner of one of these underperforming websites, you may be sitting on a goldmine. You just need the proper tools and knowledge to extract that gold.

At the end of this report I will present you with an opportunity to receive a free, no-obligation website audit and opportunity analysis. During this conversation we will thoroughly review your website, the opportunities that exist in your market, and what it would take to make your website a valuable resource that drives new customers and profits to your business.

The Direct Response Website: Your Key to Online Gold

We've already established that you need a website, but not just any website... You need a highly visible direct response website.

Understand this: The goal of a local business website is to cause your visitor to take action.

Studies show that **94% of people that visit a website never come back**. That's why it's important to have a strong call-to-action.

With that in mind, let's consider who is visiting your website and why:

- Prospects
- Customers/Clients

- Vendors/Suppliers
- Employees/Prospective Employees/Contractors
- Sales People
- Friends/Family

In this report we're talking about using a website as a business building and marketing tool, therefore we're going to focus on customers and prospects.

Since you have several different audiences coming to your local business website, and the website is marketing local products and services, it's unlikely you are going to make an immediate sale. Your prospects and customers are typically researching your business, looking for a phone number, address, email, or other information.

If you miss the call-to-action you've exponentially increased your chances of never seeing that visitor again... At least for the purpose of their current goal.

Capturing Visitor Contact Information

Most often your primary objective is to have your prospects and customers come to your business with money to spend. But you need to have a strong secondary objective, too, and that is to collect your visitor contact information. This is done through the use of an Automated Lead Capture System.

Not capturing prospect and customer information is one of the most common and most costly mistakes that businesses make. A strong Direct Response Website with a Automated Lead Capture System makes this task much easier and more effective for you.

Few business owners understand that there is incredible technology available that allows them to automate the process of performing personalized follow up to members of their prospect and customer list. An Automated Lead Capture System makes it possible to get your offers, sales, and other news in front of your customers very quickly... Usually in under 5 minutes. It also allows you to make a good impression on new prospects and customers by providing fast, professional responses to their requests for information about your business.

These notifications are generally in the form of email newsletters that deliver education and other value to your prospects and customers. This automation aspect is the greatest benefit of an Automated Lead Capture System, and it ensures your message and information gets delivered to your prospects and customers.

When you focus your efforts on getting website visitors to take action and register on your properly configured Automated Lead Capture System, your website becomes a Direct Response Website. If the goal of your website is to increase sales, profits, and market share for your business, you must have a Direct Response Website.

Remember, there are more and more local prospects and customers actively searching for local businesses.

If you don't have a good direct response website in place, I hope your competitors don't either.

When you take advantage of my free website audit and opportunity analysis, I'll show you this tool in action.

Search Engine Marketing (SEM)

Search engines drive more traffic to websites than all other mediums combined. If you're not showing up on the first page of the search engine's results for your keywords, then you're not in front of your target market when they're looking for you... And someone else is.

There are three ways to get traffic from search engines, and this is called Search Engine Marketing (SEM). These three methods are:

1. Organic (Search Engine Optimization, or SEO)

2. Local Business Results (SEO)

3. Pay Per Click (PPC)

There's also something else you need to understand: To get traffic and conversion, your website needs to be designed for both the search engines (algorithms), AND for humans.

The Eyes of the Search Engines

Spiders are all over the world-wide-web. These spiders are search engines (bots) that constantly crawl the internet searching what's out there on the ever-changing web.

Search engine spiders will eventually crawl your website and put your site in their index. Being indexed allows your website to be considered for search engine results and rankings. It can take spiders anywhere from a few minutes to several months to make it to a new website, and there are several factors that influence when and how often your website is crawled.

Ideally your website will be crawled every one or two weeks. Even though there is no direct correlation, a website that is crawled on a frequent basis usually ranks higher in search engine results. That's why news websites such as CNN rank so well. On the CNN website, content is changing every hour, so they are regarded as an authority on updated content. Therefore, their website is crawled several times each day. Your goal is to have a well-optimized website that is crawled frequently, even though you won't be changing content very often.

Being Found

Once you have a website, now you need to be found by the search engines. The search engine that crawls your website must be able to properly identify the website. And because search engines cannot "read" a picture or graphic, it identifies you through text on the page. The search engine's spiders can read certain tags embedded in an image (ALT tags), but because these tags can be manipulated by humans, its value to the search engine is not very high.

Search engine spiders also read other aspects of your website, such as the programming code. Therefore, your code should include metatags, which are bits of HTML code that provide information about a webpage, but are not viewable when the webpage is displayed on a browser. The most popular metatags to include are description tags and keyword tags. Some of the search engines don't index these tags, but some do. You should use metatags, but do not abuse them by stuffing your tags with keywords, which can get you penalized in your search engine rankings. You should use clear, concise descriptions and keywords directly related to your business.

Conversion Comes From Viewers

Far too often a website is designed with the search engines in mind, rather than the potential customer who is visiting your site. But because the goal of your website is to get prospects and customers to respond to your call-to-action, the proper design of a website and its content should always cater to the human visitor.

Remember, the search engine's goal is to replicate human thought and behavior, delivering the most relevant search results to a web surfer.

Many people and Search Engine Optimization companies try to trick the search engine algorithms into giving them better rankings. While this can produce short-term benefits, understand that the search engines have a responsibility to their customers to produce quality search results. If they discover you trying to manipulate your rankings, your site could be penalized, or even banned.

Good Guys Wear White

In old western movies, good guys always wore the white hats, and bad guys wore black hats. White Hat and Black Hat are also used to describe certain tactics used in the online marketing world.

Everyone is familiar with the term "spam" email. That is an example of a Black Hat marketing technique. Another example would be using techniques disapproved of by the search engines with the goal of increasing rankings. When you try to fool the search engines, you're using Black Hat marketing.

Again, the search engine's goal is to provide searchers with the most relevant results. For this reason, how they determine if a webpage is relevant is very important. Search engines don't like to be fooled, so the algorithm they use is constantly changing, making it very difficult to completely understand what is needed to rank in the top spots.

That's why you need to focus your online marketing efforts on White Hat tactics. While Black Hat methods can get you short-term results, White Hat has greater long-term potential because it conforms to the guidelines set by the online community who represent paying customers to your online business.

Search Engine Marketing Success Factors

The factors that determine how well you rank in the search engines can be divided into two categories:

1.   On-Page Factors

2.   Off-Page Factors

It is estimated that about 30% of the weight of your ranking comes from on-page factors (content, code, etc.), and 70% comes from off-page factors (link reputation, popularity, etc.).

While this report is not a comprehensive manual on Search Engine Optimization, I will briefly touch on these factors.

Organic Search Engine Optimization

Currently there is incredible opportunity in the local Search Engine Optimization (SEO) market place, but you can expect competition to increase in the upcoming years. Now is the time to jump on this opportunity so you can gain momentum and have your competitors playing "catch up" over the next few years.

While both on- and off-page factors are important for organic search engine optimization, on-page factors are the foundation of a marketing-savvy site. As such, these should be completed before moving on to off-page factors. Remember, the objective is to get your website ready and set up properly to adhere to published and tested guidelines set by the search engines.

These on-page factors include:

- **Keyword Research** – this is the process of finding and researching the search terms people enter into the search engines when conducting a search for your products or services. This is the most important task in your online marketing initiative.

- **Keyword Map Strategy** – this process involves taking the keywords you choose to focus on and mapping them to specific pages on your website.

- **On-Page Strategy** – this is how you actually build your web pages.

Organic Search and Link Building

Off-page factors, which are referred to as inbound links and backlinks, play a significant role in SEO.

One of the most important aspects of internet marketing is getting links to your business website listed on other sites with high levels of local traffic, thus giving you the opportunity to be seen by local customers and make local sales.

Links can be thought of as friends of your website. The search engines evaluate how popular you are by how many reputable friends that you have. The more reputable friends, the better your rankings will be.

Think of inbound links as endorsements to your website from other sites. These other sites are recommending your web pages to their visitors. Search engines believe that good websites will have other sites linking to them, so...

If you want better search engine rankings, acquire inbound links.

There are local directories on the internet that showcase local businesses of particular areas. These are excellent resources because local directories tend to be used by people struggling to find what they're looking for. So if your site is listed properly in the right categories, then you'll be found by those searching for your products and services.

Pay Per Click Advertising

With Pay Per Click (PPC) advertising you pay high-traffic websites (or search engines) to post your advertisement on their site, and pay them each time a visitor clicks on your ad.

PPC is based on the search term entered by the visitor, which is matched to the keywords you choose to advertise with. The theory is that visitors performing the search are rewarded with advertising specific to their needs, and the advertiser is exposed to visitors looking for exactly what they are selling.

So why would you want to spend your marketing budget on Pay Per Click advertising with the major search engines?

PPC can provide you with several important things:

- **Targeted Traffic** – your ads are shown only when visitors search for the terms you choose.

- **Geographically Targeted Traffic** – as a local business, you can (and should) set you campaign to be seen only in a specific region.

- **Quick Traffic** – you can create a campaign and the ads can be showing in just a few minutes.

- **Testing Your Keywords** – you don't really know which of the keywords you choose will pull high-converting visitors until you test them with your target audience. With PPC you can find which keywords work best for you, and then invest your time and energy optimizing your website for the keywords that convert best.

- **High Conversion Rates** – in a recent study by comScore, the conversion rate for PPC traffic was significantly higher than that of SEO traffic. This is probably because PPC traffic can be very targeted.

Ideally you would use both Pay Per Click and Organic search in your online marketing strategy, but this may not be possible due to budgetary constraints or lack of expertise. Trying to do both with insufficient resources can result in not getting results from either activity, so I recommend focusing on one or the other. And since the majority of users click on organic listings, I almost always recommend focusing your efforts on SEO over PPC.

The Power of Local Search

The most popular way for someone to find a website or web page is by going through a search engine. Google is the most popular search engine, receiving over 80% of all online searches, so it's more important to focus on getting results with them than it is with the other search engines.

Search engines and search engine users have become much more sophisticated over the past few years. In the early days people would use short "keywords" and phrases to find the websites and information they needed. A searcher may have simply typed the phrase "New Orleans Real Estate" into a search engine, checked out the first few results, and then decided on which site to visit.

These days web surfers are much better at using search engines, so keywords and keyword phrases have progressively become longer in order to return more relevant results. For example, instead of just typing in the keyword phrase of "New Orleans Real Estate", they may search for something more specific, such as "New Orleans Low Price Houses."

This mentality and the technology to support these searches has revitalized local business website and online marketing strategy. No longer are people just searching for a product or service, they now search for a niche product or service in a particular area. Instead of massive chains dominating the search results, small business websites are flourishing.

With more buyers using local searches, you need to focus your internet marketing to specific geographically-targeted (geo-targeted) keywords and areas. If you fail to do this, you'll be competing with the major players in your industry nationally, and that's a battle very difficult to win.

Local Search = Ready Buyers

Perhaps the most important thing for you to understand about local searchers is that they take action. These local searchers (customers) are usually in the latter stages of their purchasing decisions.

Suppose someone goes to a search engine and types in the search term "brake repair." What information does the search engine return? Everything from do-it-yourself repair information to big national chains that offer brake repair services.

But if someone types in a geographically-targeted search term such as "Baton Rouge brake repair", it's much more likely that they need a local, Baton Rouge business to repair their brakes.

When local prospects search for products or services in their area, they most likely have clear intentions and are ready to take action. They call, make in-store visits, and even send email to the businesses they feel can assist them.

There are over 1 billion local searches performed online every month, and this rate is growing by 50% each year (Google).

Google understands the importance of local searches and the growing trend in its use, and it's made evident by their display of up to ten local searches within their organic listings.

In April 2009, Google brought local business search results into the mainstream organic search results without adding a geographical modifier to the search. At the time of this writing, Google is getting even more aggressive in regard to local search and local maps. They understand that local search plays a major role in the future of their company... And the future of the internet.

Take a look at some recent market data supporting this position:

- 74% of all internet users regularly perform local searches (The Kelsey Group).

- 82% of local searchers follow up offline via an in-store visit, phone call, or purchase (comScore Networks).

- More people now use internet search engines to seek out local merchants than the yellow pages and white pages combined (TMP Directional Marketing).

- 70% of all US households use the internet when shopping locally for products and services (The Kelsey Group & comStat).

- Local searches have increased by 76% between February 2007 and February 2008. Additionally, the number of searches per searcher has increased from approximately 6.5 to 11.3 during the same period of time (comScore Networks).

Getting Found in Local Searches

People use the internet in many different ways, and it's impossible to capture every single person in your area looking for a product or service like yours. However, you can make it very easy for searchers to find your business by being prominent in multiple areas of the web.

Internet marketing is essentially about being "found" online by your target market. They are looking for what you're selling, so you have to make it as easy as possible for them to find you.

With so many different types of content and various ways of receiving information on the internet, there are limitless possibilities for marketing your website. Whether this is in the form of local business directories, online classified ads, or videos about your product posted on popular websites, you're sure to find people who are looking for your products and services.

Social Media

Social media is the method used on the internet for people to share and discuss information. The term "social media marketing" refers to internet-based communication with social media sites to promote a business, product or service. These social media channels use communication as a means to generate word-of-mouth advertising, listen to customer demands, and analyze customer behaviors.

Social media is still fairly new to the internet. In fact, it was only in spring of 2009 that Twitter became a household name.

Typically local business is slow to follow new trends (building websites, using email, etc.), but social media for local business is being adopted at a much quicker rate than past technologies.

At a media conference in 2004, Tim O'Reilly coined the term Web 2.0. Web 2.0 isn't a new internet; it refers to shifting times and the major changes that have taken place for business since its inception.

Social Media Marketing (SMM) is essentially creating word-of-mouth advertising in an electronic form using Web 2.0 sites like Twitter, Facebook, and LinkedIn.

If you want to get the most exposure from Social Media Marketing, you must provide your market with unique and valuable content. This strategy can drive an enormous amount of traffic from Web 2.0 sites by providing links pointing to the pages you want to promote. Therefore, it should be an integral part of your strategy, bringing everything together on the internet for your business.

There are three basic categories of Social Media Marketing websites:

1. Social Networking & Communication Sites

2. Social Collaboration Sites

3. Social Bookmarking Sites

Social Networking and Communication

There are dozens of social networking websites, and they include some of the biggest and fastest growing sites on the internet, such as Facebook and MySpace. I've even heard reputable experts say that social networking is bigger than the internet itself.

Social Collaboration Sites

The concept of social collaboration websites is "a collaboration of information to leverage a synergy among a mass of people." Wikipedia is the world's largest online encyclopedia that is built by its users. Opinion websites such as Epinions are places where people state their views about products or services.

Social Bookmarking Sites

Social bookmarking is a way for people to search, store, manage, and organize bookmarks of web pages on the internet. You're probably familiar with the bookmark (or favorites) feature on your internet browser. It allows navigation to the pages you bookmark with just one click. Social bookmarking takes that feature and makes your bookmarks available on the internet, so when you're not at your normal computer, you still have access to all of your stored web pages.

At the time of this writing, 10 of the top 20 most visited websites in the US included social media sites. I have heard that there are over 600,000 new subscribers to Facebook every day, and that if Facebook were a country, it would be the 4th largest country in the world.

Twittering – Do You Tweet?

The typical first response I get when discussing Twitter is "I don't get it." In fact, in mid-2009 I saw a statistic floating around the web claiming that 60% of Twitter users don't get its concept, and leave within the first month.

Twitter is a micro-blogging website that allows people to make status updates of 140 characters or less. These are called "tweets." Many people argue that Twitter is a dying fad, and that there is no real business application to this new means of communication.

But there are many businesses that disagree, including Naked Pizza in New Orleans, LA. Within the first month of applying the application to their business, their sales soared 20% due to its Twitter presence. As of June 2009, Naked Pizza had about 4,300 followers, and have had Twitter advertising blitzes that accounted for 69% of their daily sales.

It is hard to fathom the value of social sites and how they are changing our lives. There are over 3.3 billion cell phone subscriptions in the world… that's over half of the world's population. Web 2.0 is being designed to work on mobile devices.

Web Video

Online video is one of the best means of connecting to your target market. Our brains seek out sensory experiences, and on the internet video is the best way to do it. Video creators can communicate messages on multiple levels through visual imagery, spoken words, music, and visual text.

As a small business, you can use web video to engage your customers and make stronger, more personal connections. Imagine your competitors selling with text on their antiquated website while you're using video to speak directly to your customers. You can look right at them, in your own real voice and tell them the advantages of working with you.

If you think about it, video is perfect for local small businesses. Why do people choose small businesses over the larger chains anyway? Because you're reliable, friendly, provide great service, and they develop a relationship with you. Video augments all those attributes that make you special to your customers. It's what your customers are looking for.

Video also offers another huge advantage on the web. Video has a huge potential to reach a massive audience for your small business, and this strategy alone can help you dominate the entire front page of Google. Online video can help you reach a large local audience for a minimal investment, providing incredible ROI.

I would like to end this section on web video with several ideas of how you could put web video to use for your local business.

- Demonstrate how your products and services work.

- Create training videos on how to properly use your products.

- Interview customers to capture testimonials and success stories.

- Interview employees as they discuss what they do and how they help customers.

- Record a greeting from the owner or CEO of the company.

- Use video as a Call-To-Action on your sales pages and in email campaigns.

- Add video to your Google Maps profile, Facebook Fan Page, and LinkedIn profile.

- Record FAQs with real prospects and customers asking the questions.

- Interview your key strategic business partners and referral sources.

- Create all types of "how-to" videos to help demonstrate your expertise.

- Create a contest and reward your customers for creating their own videos promoting your business or products and services.

Targeted Email Marketing

Email marketing is a form of direct marketing that uses email as a means of communicating messages to an audience that has asked for those messages.

The key word in the above sentence is "asked", because if they haven't asked for the messages, then it is considered spam. When I suggest using email, know that I'm suggesting sending email to targeted lists of prospects and customers who have "asked" to receive information from you.

Employing a targeted email marketing program is critical to the success of your online marketing initiative. Not only is it cost effective, but it can be very lucrative, and it will help you build your prospect and customer list (which can become your most valuable business asset).

Don't make the mistake of only sending out solicitations and offers when you start your email marketing campaign. If you do, you risk aggravating the people on your list, and many will unsubscribe. Your objective is to build a relationship with your prospects and customers, and to do this with email you must offer valuable content to them first. This is how you build trust and credibility, which is necessary to drive future sales.

A web searcher who finds you over the internet doesn't really know you. You don't have the same credibility as you would if they would have come into your brick and mortar store, looked at your products or talked to your associates about your services. You must let these people get to know and trust you.

Remember the Automated Lead Capture System I mentioned in the section of this report titled Local Business Websites That Work? It makes this process much easier, allowing you to set up your initial emails to go out automatically over a predetermined period of time. You can let your prospects get to know things about you, your business, and maybe even your family. You should also give them some free information that will be helpful to them in some way. If you do these things first, when you do ask them to buy something, they are much more likely to do so.

Will the Internet Work for You?

In this chapter I have shown you many of the opportunities that exist for local businesses to find new customers on the internet. Local internet marketing is at the beginning of a growth phase that all major internet players recognize, but only a few local companies have taken advantage of. The time to capitalize on this opportunity has never been better.

As a business owner and entrepreneur myself, I know the question you're asking yourself: **"Can I make local internet marketing work for my business?"**

At this point, there is only one honest answer I can give you: I don't know, but it's very likely.

I have a great way for you to find out for yourself using data about your business category and local marketplace from the most reputable and undisputable source of information on the internet: Google.

First, navigate your web browser to Google.com. If you are reading this report in PDF format, just click on this link: www.Google.com.

Do a search for the term "keyword tool" and click on the "I'm Feeling Lucky" button. The Google Adwords Keyword Tool should come up. If for some reason it doesn't, here is the URL: https://adwords.google.com/select/KeywordToolExternal

Step 1: Keyword Research

For our purposes, the keyword research is going to be quick and easy. This is not at all supposed to be thorough keyword research. The only objective at this point is to determine what type of activity exists in the local area for your business and acquire traffic estimates.

Your keyword research for a local business starts with two components:

1. Geographical Modifier

2. Core Term

The geographical modifier is a word or phrase to describe the geographical area, such as the city name, state, zip code, or possibly a city nickname (New

Orleans = NOLA). In most cases you will find the greatest search volume with the city or zip code.

The core term refers to the product, service, or the phrase that is likely to be used when searching for your product or service. I'll give you a few examples:

Theme/Product/Service	Core Term
Dentist	Dentist
	Root canal
	Dental
	Oral surgeon
	Teeth whitening
Realtor	Realtor
	Real estate
	Real estate agent
Defense Attorney	Defense attorney
	Lawyer
	Attorney
	Criminal attorney
Delivery Company	Courier
	Courier service
	Courier services
	Messenger service
	Delivery company
	Courier company

Note: This is not to be mistaken as a full list of core terms. Each theme could be expanded to several hundred terms and this exercise is not intended to teach thorough keyword research.

Now go to the keyword tool and put in one of the core terms for your business along with your geographical modifier. Start with the city your business is looking to grow in.

For this example, I'm going to use the term "Dentist" in the town I live in, "Baton Rouge."

Notice the numbers? With one core term and one geographical modifier, we now have proof that two keyword phrases (Baton Rouge Dentist + Baton Rouge Dentists) has a combined search volume of 6,400 searches.

The number in the Local Search Volume section indicates the number of searches performed in the Baton Rouge area.

Because we are using just two core terms (and there are dozens more to choose from), and only one geographical modifier (there are several suburbs and nearby towns/cities you could include), we could easily brainstorm many more search terms. So it would be safe to assume you could easily double the number seen here if you were to use all of those search terms.

Based on this data, the new total would be around 12,000 monthly searches.

Ultimately, the average local business has a keyword list of around 30 terms. The reason I use this number is that I have found that it's possible for the average local business to have around 15 essential pages ranked in the search engines.

Since a single page should not be optimized for more than three keywords (ideally two keywords), I estimate that the total keyword list for SEO purposes will be around 30. Note: This quick formula does not apply to PPC.

The above research provides evidence that just one of those terms has 6,000 searches a month.

Now let's compute a daily average. In most cases, divide your number of monthly searches by 21. This will give you a daily average. I choose to use 21 days in a month because most businesses are open 21 days a month, and search volume tends to drop significantly over weekends. If your clients require service on the weekend, feel free to modify this number and use 30 days.

12,000 / 21 = 571 daily searches for "Baton Rouge Dentist!"

Summary

As you've discovered throughout this report, the internet has taken over as the dominant way buyers find local business. The good news is that with an intelligent and systematic approach, you can have a great advantage over your competition in the information age... but you need to embrace this exciting new media now.

All of the data and statistics tell you everything you need to know. Being that local search has only become popular in the last few years, it's likely to grow even more in the future.

But use caution! Building and maintaining a successful direct response website and online marketing strategy that helps you create and maintain new customers is no simple task. A productive website and marketing system demand constant attention and they must remain flexible enough to change as quickly as the latest internet and web-based technologies.

So unless you have advanced skills in website development and online marketing techniques, you're better off allowing a professional to create, configure, maintain, and manage any comprehensive online marketing programs you choose to undertake.

The money you spend creating new and repeat customers is an investment to your business, so making the right decision regarding this matter will save you time, money and frustration.

Chapter 4 Notes

_____

_____

_____

_____

_____

_____

_____

_____

_____

_____

_____

_____

Chapter 5: The Most Ignored Marketing Strategy

You're in business to make money, and undoubtedly you've worked hard to find and convert prospects into clients. This white paper is about a marketing strategy that will make all your hard work pay off at a much higher level.

Inside this chapter you will learn how to use this strategy to:

- Dramatically increase the return on your marketing investment.

- Greatly reduce your marketing costs.

- Make selling your products and services up to 16-times easier.

- How a simple 5% improvement in a key growth area can result in an additional 20-40% increase in profitability.

Read this carefully and with your own business in mind. Use the open outside margins to take notes relevant to your specific situation, and then prepare to put this strategy into action and reap the rewards of achieving new milestones in sales and profitability.

Introduction

A recent newspaper article titled "Everyone Wants to Be a Millionaire", discussed the obsession Americans have with becoming wealthy. In fact, our fixation on becoming a "millionaire" has reached nearly pandemic proportions, according to one psychologist…. even though a $1 million dollars isn't what it used to be.

For instance, if you had $1 million in 1980, it would be the same as having more than $2 million today. And in 1970, $1 million was worth 4.4 times what it is now. Moreover, people who win a million or more through lotteries, casinos and the like, never take home the entire amount, thanks to state and federal taxes.

But that doesn't seem to matter to most people. "What we have is the dream of making it big," says Mark Alch, author of *"How to Become a Millionaire: A Straightforward Approach to Accumulating Wealth."* "People still think a seven-digit figure is an extreme amount of money."

And it is a lot of money to most people… there's no question about it. But how does one go about obtaining that kind of money? And what are the best, quickest, least risky ways to do it?

What It Takes To Make A Million Dollars

In the same article, USA TODAY analyst Danny Sheridan calculated the odds against making $1 million by these methods:

- Inheriting $1 million: 12 million to 1

- Winning the lottery: 12 million to 1

- Playing the slots in a casino: 6 million to 1

- Winning a game show: 4 million to 1

- Saving $800 a month for 30 years: 1.5 million to 1

- Working for a company that goes public: 10,000 to 1

- Owning a small business: 1,000 to 1

Besides the obvious tax write-offs and deductions a business affords its owners, there are other highly-leverageable advantages, as well.

It's true that businesses have expenses... operating expenses such as rent, utilities, telephones, business supplies, equipment and wages and commissions. In addition, they may have expenses relating to production, manufacturing or product costs. And of course, there's the cost of promoting or marketing the products or services the business sells.

Of all the costs incurred by the business, the only one that truly is not a cost (other than perhaps, land or facility appreciation), is the costs incurred in marketing. **You see, marketing should not be viewed as a cost or an expense... It's the best investment in the growth of your business you can make.**

The Most Profitable Business Investment You Can Make

Let's suppose you invest in stocks, bonds or mutual funds. What kind of return can you reasonably expect to make? 5 %? 10%? 15%? Maybe. And if you're really lucky... maybe 20 or 25%.

But along with those numbers, comes a certain amount of risk. You could very easily lose it all in the process.

But an effective marketing campaign could have the potential of generating up to 5,000% or more in profits. If you spend, say, $100 on an ad or a campaign and it returns $1,000 in profits, you've just earned 10 times your ROI (Return On Investment). That's a 1,000% return. And if it were to return $5,000 in profits... you'd have a 5,000% return.

I can hear your questions now. "How realistic is it to invest $100 and get a $1,000 or a $5,000 return? Does it ever really happen? And if it does, is it the exception rather than the rule?"

Good questions. All of them. And the answer is... Yes, it is realistic. Yes it does happen. And yes, it is the exception rather than the rule.

Now, don't let my answer to that last question (the exception rather than the rule) dissuade or discourage you. It doesn't have to be that way. But the truth is that...

The newspaper, the magazine, the TV or radio station, or the mail carrier doesn't care what's on your ad or in your letter... they're going to deliver the message (whatever it is) to the intended recipient. And if you get one response, 100 responses, or even 1,000 responses, the ad or letter costs are all the same.

It's not how much you spend on the ad that counts. It's not even which media you choose that solely determines your response rate (although choosing effective media is important). More than anything, it's what you do or say in your ad or letter… the trust and credibility you build with the reader, and the offer you make, that will determine the response you get.

And if that's the case, why not make the very best offer to those who you've already developed a high level of trust and credibility with, so that you can maximize the return on your investment? I'm talking about your current and past customers. Those who have already experienced doing business with you and are familiar with how you operate. Those who have enjoyed the benefits of your products and services.

All the research shows that…

It Costs Six Times More To Get A Prospect To Buy From You Than It Does To Resell To An Existing Client.

Acquiring new customers is costly, and in many cases, the money earned on the first sale doesn't even cover the acquisition costs. In fact, many studies have shown that it costs six times more to get a new customer than it does to keep an existing one, and that **it's 16 times easier to sell to an existing customer than to a new one.**

That said, why would any astute business owner, manager, salesperson or entrepreneur even let the thought of spending a minute of time or a dime of their resources on attracting new customers before doing all they can to squeeze every last ounce of business out of their existing or past customers or clients?

The truth is, **the real money – your profits – comes from the additional sales of the products and services that you make to your customers on the "back end."**

If you happen to sell a limited number of products or services to your customers, or sell to them on an infrequent basis, or if what you sell can be duplicated by another product or service offered by a competitor, your business can only achieve a fraction of its potential.

Why Should Your Market Do Business With You?

If you really want your business to be as successful as it can be, to thrive and not just survive, and to maximize the investment you've made in it, you've got to continually find ways to offer your customers unique advantages they can't get anywhere else.

And when you do, you'll gain your customers' loyalty, motivate them to do more business with you, keep them as customers for a long time, and inspire them to tell their other business associates and friends about you.

In other words, if you can give your customers unique, compelling and profitable reasons to do business with you over and over again, they'll not only keep you in business, they'll make you incredibly wealthy and successful in the process.

Your existing or past clients or customers have already had at least one buying experience with you, so they are familiar with you. And if you've done your job well and made them feel special, the likelihood of them doing business with you again is greatly enhanced. Trust and credibility have already been established. Now all you need to do is make them an enticing offer.

On the other hand, new prospects… those who haven't had the same buying experience with you, require much more time, effort and money to bring them to the same point of trust as your current clients.

You first have to get your new prospect's attention. You do that with ads, sales letters, newsletters, postcards, telemarketing campaigns and a variety of other types of media. Then you nurture them, hold their hand, and walk them step-by-step through the trust-building phase just to get them to the level of trust that your current customers were at when they began doing business with you.

You have to lead them up the Loyalty Ladder, from Suspect to Prospect, then on to Shopper, and eventually to Customer, Client, Advocate and finally, to Raging Fan. All this takes time and money. But you have to do it, because…

The average business loses between 20-40% of its client base each year. This means that you must get 10-20% more new clients each year just to stay even!

This one simple fact... this single statement explains why so many businesses are struggling today. And why they spend so much time, effort and money trying to attract new clients to do business with them.

Now, most business owners are good technicians. That is, they know how to effectively produce or acquire the products they sell. And if they run their businesses fairly efficiently, they manage to get by. But they do it at a level far below where they could and should be operating.

Getting New Business Is Not Something Most Business Owners Are Proficient In

The cold, hard fact is most business owners, most professionals, most entrepreneurs, most managers, most salespeople, most people responsible for getting new customers for their business enterprise, simply don't know how to get those new customers on an effective or cost-efficient basis. So they depend on ad agencies or media sales reps from magazines, newspapers, radio and TV stations to design their business-getting tools for them. And the truth be known, most of those reps or sales people don't have a clue as to how to create marketing campaigns that produce measurable results on a cost-effective basis.

Getting new customers is not just important, it's critical. You simply have to do it, especially if your business is losing 20% of your customers to attrition each year.

But getting new customers through traditional means is only one of many ways to grow your business to the point where you're earning the kind of profits and income that you want. There are other things you can do that are not only more effective, but are more cost-efficient as well.

The Reality of Retention

Listen to this exciting statistic…

For every 5% increase in customer retention, you can generate an additional 30-40% increase in profitability over 12-16 months.

Think about that for a minute. If your business is like most, and you lose 20% of your customers each year, that means that 80% stay with you and continue to do business with you. But if you were to increase that number to 86 percent, you could enjoy a 30 to 40 percent increase in profitability.

Remember, that it costs 6 times more to get a new customer than it does to keep an existing one, and it's 16 times easier to sell to an existing customer than to a new one.

When you compare the acquisition costs for getting new customers to like you, know you, trust you, and buy from you the first time, versus getting your existing customers to repurchase from you, the cost-to-sale difference is significantly different.

So how do you increase your customer retention? How do you get them to buy from you again and again? How do you get your customers to continue doing business with you year after year, until they no longer have any need for your products or services? And how do you get them to refer others to you so your acquisition costs come down below, way below, the six times figure? What are the most efficient and most cost-effective ways to do those things?

Cater to Peoples' Differences, And You'll Win Customers for Life

People are all different… But they're really all the same. How can that be?

People all want to be viewed as different, special, unique. They want to feel as though their needs are different than anyone else's, that the answers to their problems are different than their neighbor's, and that they require special attention and special solutions.

Dr. Murry Banks, the popular New York psychologist, says that all buying springs out of four basic motives or wants:

1. To live longer and better

2. A feeling of importance – respect, power, prestige, admiration

3. To be appreciated

4. A desire for variety or change

Even though people all view themselves as different, they are really the same in that the four buying motives appeal to everyone.

With regard to motive number two, Dr. Banks cites the example of a little boy at the pool who shouts to his mom, "Watch me, mom, watch me!"

And while grown-ups don't act in the same manner as the little boy, they do the same thing with their big cars, furniture, homes, jewelry, etc. There's really not much difference between children and adults… just in the methods.

Understanding human nature is critical if you're in business. Once you understand what your customers' wants are, you can become a "Want Creator", rather than a "Needs Satisfier."

And when you become the one Want Creator with the only logical and viable solution to your prospects' and customers' wants, you've just set yourself up for unlimited success. Not only that, you have effectively eliminated your competition and are on the road to becoming the dominating force in your marketplace.

Knowing, and Then Selling to a Prospect's Or Customer's Needs Is a Sure Way to Success

Let's take a look at your business enterprise. When someone does business with you the first time, what happens during the transaction? Do you just sell them the product or service they came to buy? Or do you find out more about them? What their business is. How they intend on using the item they purchased. What other related products or services they might need or be interested in. How many family members, employees or associates they may have that might enjoy the same benefits those products or services provides.

What about any other important or pertinent information that you can use later on to help create additional purchases from them or referrals of their associates? The more complete and comprehensive the information in your customer database is, the more you can target their individual needs according to the four basic motives, and the more closely you can tailor your correspondence to them and their feeling of being "different" than anyone else.

A good place to begin if you don't already have a system in place, is by looking over the "MacKay 66," found in Harvey MacKay's great book, "*Swim With The Sharks Without Being Eaten Alive.*"

You don't have to go to the extent that MacKay went to and use all 66 questions, but his list will at least give you a starting point to develop your own list of critical questions. Once you have this information and have entered it into your database, you've got to do something with it. It's not enough just to have it. You must use it.

"Love 'em and Leave 'em"… An All Too Familiar Scenario

It's a fact. Not a pretty one, but a fact just as well. It's happened to me. It's happened to you. It's happened to my customers. And it's happened to yours. In fact, it's happened to everyone who has ever made a purchase from someone else, or from some company, whether they be big or small.

What I'm referring to, is the old, "Love 'em and leave 'em" scenario. You know how it goes: companies spend tons of money advertising to Suspects with the hopes of finding a few Prospects… people who might be a candidate for what the company is offering. Eventually some of those Prospects become Shoppers, then a few of those Shoppers hopefully end up as Customers.

Then an amazing thing happens. The customer leaves with his or her purchase and the company goes about trying to attract more Suspects, beginning the process all over again.

You see, the business "Loved 'em" enough to get them to purchase one time, then "Left 'em"… never to contact that customer again. And if they did happen to contact them, it was most likely a lame, weak and ineffective attempt to sell them what the company wanted to sell… not what the customer might want.

The Most Underused Marketing Tool

Now let me introduce to you the most effective, most cost-efficient, most profitable thing you can do in your business, and that is to create a database of your current and past customers and properly follow up with them.

It doesn't have to be an elaborate system, plan or strategy, and it doesn't have to be costly. But it does have to be well thought-out, planned and tailored to the unique wants of your customers, if you want it to be overwhelmingly successful.

Believe me when I say this: This one strategy is the most overlooked, yet most effective marketing tool you have in your arsenal for getting your customers to buy from you more often, extending their buying lifetime with you, and getting them to refer others to you.

This one strategy can do more for building your business than just about anything else you can do… And it can do it in record time!

And if you fail to do this? It'll cost you thousands and thousands of dollars in lost business and profits.

Your Three Levels of Customers

An effective follow-up strategy is concerned with three sources of customers…

1. Existing Customers
2. Past Customers
3. Potential Customers or Prospects

Existing Customers… The Most Powerful Source of Profits Any Business Has

All things being equal, people will do business with people they like, they know, and they trust. All things being unequal, people will still do business with people they like, they know and they trust.

And since it costs up to six times more to get a new customer to like you, know you and trust you enough to buy from you, it just makes sense to spend most of your time, effort and money strengthening the relationships you already have with your existing customers.

Here are a few things to consider when developing a system for following up with your existing customers or clients…

Determine the number of times you want to contact your clients, and over what period of time. You want them to know that you're thinking of them and that you have something of value to say to them. But the last thing you want to do is bug them to death. You might, for instance, decide that you want to contact them six times in the next 12 months.

Determine the frequency of contacts. In the example in step one, you decided on six contacts over a 12-month period. Now, you want to determine how often you'll contact them. Will it be every other month for the entire year? Or will it be once a month for the first three months, then once every three months thereafter? Or, if your customers have a product that expires or renews, such as an insurance policy, will you increase the number of contacts you make just prior to their renewal?

Determine the method of contact. There are a couple of considerations here. First, what is the method of contact that has the greatest chance of attracting their attention? Next, what method is the most cost-effective? And third, what method of contact would provide the greatest likelihood of them responding? Are postcards the best? What about letters, faxes, newsletters or email? What if you were to send an audio or video cassette, or make telephone calls or in-person visits? Each of these methods of contact has inherent costs and response-predictors, and should be weighed very carefully before cranking out any new contact campaign.

Determine the purpose of the contact. Why are you contacting them? Is it to thank them for buying from you? Is it to make them an offer on new merchandise or other services they may have a need for? Is it to ask for referrals? Remember, you should know each of your customers and what their dominant buying motives are. You should know what they've purchased in the past and what they're likely to respond to in the future. No sense wasting your time trying to sell someone something they have no need for, don't want, or can't use.

Determine the offer you'll make them. The offer you'll make depends a lot on who you're contacting and why you're contacting them. If you have a new product or service, or have another product or service that your customer might be interested in, you'll want to make your offer such that it will be difficult for them to refuse. Now that doesn't always mean that your prices will be lower than anyone else's. It could very well mean that this product or service will do more to help them solve or prevent a particular problem or situation better than any other alternative.

Determine how you'll reduce or eliminate any risk on the part of the customer. Whenever any product or service is sold or purchased, someone is being asked to assume part of the risk… either the customer or the business owner. It stands to reason, that if your customer is asked to bear the bulk of the risk that could have a negative impact on the chances of making a sale. On the other hand, if you are taking the lion's share of the risk, your chances of making a sale can be greatly enhanced. Determine what works out the best for the kind of product or service you're offering.

Determine what (if any) backend products or services you can offer once a purchase is made. You should always have a backend product. If what you sell is a one-time purchase and you don't have anything else you can sell your customers, then arrange with other companies who have products that are complimentary, but are non-competing with yours. Then build a joint-venture arrangement with them to offer their products to your customers and you can split the profits.

There are many other things you can do to make the selling of additional products or services to your customers more effective. And they're not difficult. It just takes a little planning, a little thought, and a little creativity. But more than anything, it takes action. You've got to act on the plans you create.

Your Past Customers… A Hidden, Forgotten and Untapped Source Of Profits

These are your past customers… those who have done business with you in the past but are no longer considered "active." They haven't purchased from you recently.

Something happened. They've quit coming back. Maybe they've outgrown their need for your products or services. Maybe they've gone to another competitor. Maybe they moved out of your marketing area. Whatever the reason, they're no longer doing business with you.

Remember, these former customers at one time liked and trusted you enough to purchase from you. It may have been a certain sale or offer that you ran. It may be that they did business with you because you were conveniently located to them. Or it may be that they were referred to you by a friend, a family member, a neighbor or a relative. Whatever the case, at one time they did indeed buy from you.

Now, just because they haven't purchased from you again recently, doesn't mean all is lost.

One of the biggest mistakes businesses make is that they fail to keep in touch with this group of customers. If you've run your business properly, they'll remember the way you did things, how you treated them, and the quality of products and services you sold them. And it won't take much to get them back to do business with you again.

But what if you didn't do things the best way? Perhaps they had a bad experience with your business or a certain person that worked for you. An apology or explanation of the circumstances and what you've done to correct the situation can do nothing but help re-solidify an old relationship.

You can use the same planning and contacting sequence that is listed above when determining how best to contact this group of customers. Whatever you do, don't let this valuable resource fall through the cracks.

If these customers left your business to go with a competitor, it won't be long before they have some type of negative experience with that competitor. It's just so rare that you find, in any type of business, industry or profession, a business that is on top of all things all the time. And most often, you'll find that nearly every business is product-oriented, and not customer-focused.

Once you "get your act together" and begin delivering more than the benefits that the products or services you sell provide, you'll find that this group of customers can turn out to be a real profit center for you.

Your Potential Customers or Prospects... Knowing Who They Are Can Make All the Difference In The World

Here's one of the most critical questions I can ask: Do you know who your best prospects are? I mean, *really* know?

Do you know who they are? Where they are? How to contact them? What kinds of needs or wants they have? What kinds of offers they respond to? What would prompt them to buy from you? What kinds of buying habits they have, and who they hang around with?

If you don't know the answers to these critical questions, you're basically just shooting in the dark. The more clearly you can focus in on a tight target market, the more success you'll have.

Think about it for a minute. What is the difference between a Suspect... just a name, and a Prospect... someone who may be in the market for your product or service and has the financial capacity to buy? The answer, of course, is all the difference in the world.

Why would you want to spend any time, effort or money trying to convince people who have no need, no want, or no capacity to buy?

The real truth is, if you're trying to sell to everyone, you're really selling to no one. But when you focus on a tightly identified niche, you can more effectively address the needs of that market and make offers that they are predisposed to take advantage of.

It's the old "Rifle vs. Shotgun" approach. If you can single out a certain market segment who is more likely to buy from you, you're way better off directing your ads and marketing efforts to them than you are the general public.

An Action Plan For Success

Here's what you can do. Once you've set up your database of your existing customers, take a good, analytical look at them.

- Determine what their buying habits are.
- See where they live or work.
- Look at what types of products or services they buy.
- What their repeat purchase patterns are.
- What types of ads they respond to.

Look at all the information that may be pertinent to your business. Does their age, family characteristics, type of home they live in or cars they drive have anything to do with how or what they buy from you? And how about the kind of work they do, or the profession they work in?

Once you've carefully analyzed your existing customers and categorized them into groups according to buying patterns, habits or interests, then look in your marketplace for other, similar groups of people or businesses.

The sources for locating these groups are numerous and can range from compiled lists, to directories, to list brokers, and a number of other resources.

Now that you've identified who your best prospects are, use the same steps outlined above for following up with your existing customers, to contact them. Follow up. Stay with it. Don't let this slip. And always be testing different offers, different guarantees, different headlines.

Be on the lookout for anything that increases your response rate. And be open to using and testing different methods of contacting them.

This group of contacts has the potential of driving your business right through the roof... if you approach them properly.

Your customers and clients—both current, past, and potential—are the greatest asset you have in your business. You've got to treat them with love and respect. You've got to let them know that you care about them, both as customers and as people.

And you've got to constantly keep in touch with them, always offering them a "better deal" (which doesn't always mean lower price), a better value, increased ways to further enhance the advantage, benefit, use or enjoyment they get from using your products and services, and from doing business with you.

Follow up with them. Don't harass or bug them. Develop a plan... an easy-to-administer plan for systematically and continuously following up, always offering your help, expertise, and the value you bring to your relationship with them beyond what the actual products or services you sell offer.

If you'll do these things, you'll be putting into motion **the most effective and neglected marketing strategy in existence.**

Chapter 5 Notes

_____

_____

_____

_____

_____

_____

_____

_____

_____

_____

_____

_____

_____

About the Author

Russ Holder is a leading business development and marketing expert and best-selling author with the life purpose of "helping companies systematically and dramatically accelerate their growth."

Through his books, speaking engagements, and consulting programs, Russ has served as a strategic advisor to leaders of high-growth businesses worldwide, including multiple members of both the Fortune and Inc. 500 lists. As the CEO and founder of TriFecta Marketing, a results-driven business development and marketing firm, Russ has helped over 200 entrepreneurs and business leaders in 40-plus industries and professions increase sales, profits and market share.

Maximizing Business Growth was published in 2010 and was an Amazon Best Seller. Based on Russ's proprietary TriFecta Exponential Growth Model, the book focuses on systematically improving the Nine Growth Keys of a business to generate powerful Marketing Synergy and exponential growth.

Visit Russ Holder on the web at www.RussHolder.com.

More from Russ Holder

Russ Holder's business development and marketing strategies have been tested worldwide for almost 20 years. With client companies ranging from small, one-person operations to some of the most successful Fortune 500 corporations, Russ's methods, systems and strategies eliminate the guesswork and financial risk associated with marketing and growing your business.

More Books by Russ Holder

- *Growing Your Business During an Economic Meltdown* (2007–ISBN: 978-1-939315-16-8)

- *Points of Failure* (2008–ISBN: 978-1-939315-17-5)

- *Maximizing Business Growth* (2010–ISBN: 978-1-939315-01-4)

- *20 Reasons Why Your Sales S*tink (2012–ISBN: 978-1-939315-02-1)

- *Going Up* (2014–ISBN: 978-1-939315-14-4)

IMPORTANT NOTE: The information in this book only scratches the surface of getting the best results from your sales and marketing efforts. Be sure to get on Russ Holder's mailing list for up-to-date information and resources to grow your business in sales, profits and market share. You can sign up at www.RussHolder.com.

www.ingramcontent.com/pod-product-compliance
Lightning Source LLC
Chambersburg PA
CBHW060045210326
41520CB00009B/1277